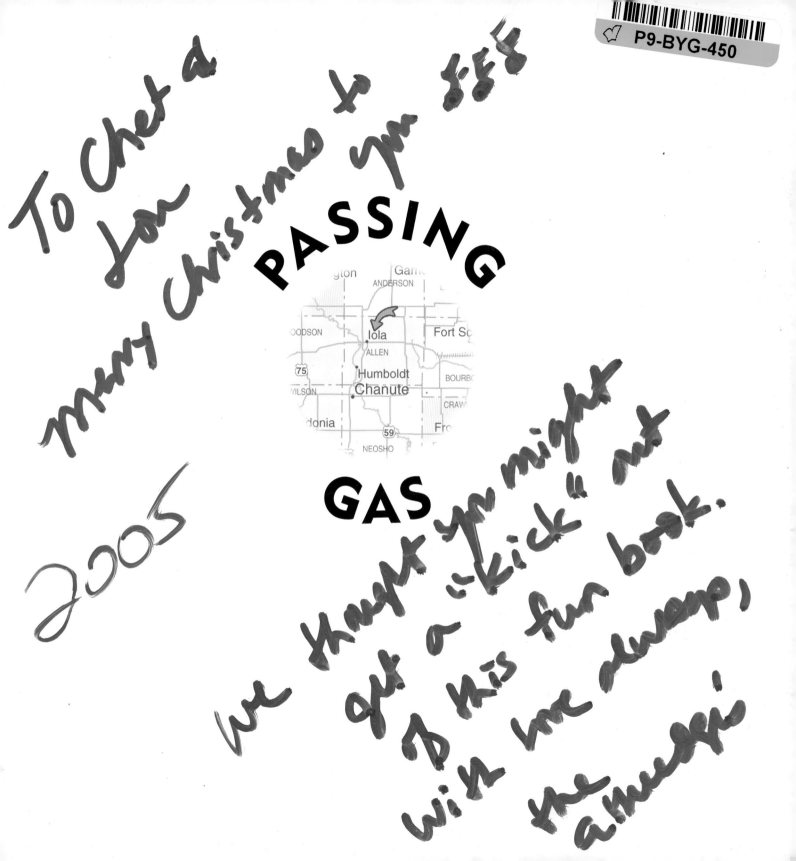

To Chet &
Lou

Merry Christmas

2005

PASSING

GAS

we thought you might
get a "kick" out
of this fun book.

with love always,

the Mudgis

PASSING GAS

And Other Towns Along the American Highway

GARY GLADSTONE

TEN SPEED PRESS

Berkeley | Toronto

🔟

Ten Speed Press
P.O. Box 7123
Berkeley, California 94707
www.tenspeed.com

Distributed in Australia by Simon and Schuster Australia, in Canada by Ten Speed Press Canada, in New Zealand by Southern Publishers Group, in South Africa by Real Books, and in the United Kingdom and Europe by Airlift Book Company.

Cover Design by Jennifer Barry Design
Text Design by Toni Tajima

To purchase fine art prints of subjects from this book visit http://www.passing-gas.com

Library of Congress Cataloging-in-Publication Data
Gladstone, Gary.
  Passing Gas : and other towns along the American highway / by Gary Gladstone.
    p. cm.
  ISBN-10: 1-58008-456-7
  ISBN-13: 978-1-58008-456-7
1. Photography, Artistic. 2. Street photography. 3. Cities and towns--United States--Pictorial works.
4. Gladstone, Gary. I. Title.
  TR654 .G566 2002
  779'.9973--dc21
                          2002007562
First printing, 2003

Printed in Hong Kong

4 5 6 7 8 9 10 — 09 08 07 06 05

For Dirty Joe, Wally Moon, and Chops—
believers who said I could really do stuff like this.

Acknowledgments

Thanks to Ella, for help in researching the obscure, and to Barry, for setting the rules about writing while retaining the fun. Special thanks to my son, Greg Gladstone, a rising computer animation star who worked after hours to make the maps in this book. (The guy has talent, what can I say?)

Also thanks to my peers, the members of the PhotoNews Network® PhotoPRO Forum, a discussion group of working professional photographers whose initial challenge and subsequent cheerleading kept this project alive long enough to become a book. Here it is guys and gals!

BEFORE THE ROAD

It was unusually quiet that Saturday morning at the upstate New York weekly newspaper where I worked part-time as a copy boy. I'd finished running proofs around town to merchant advertisers, and now I was acting busy by sorting little black-and-white photos—not the newspaper's pictures, but mine, a harvest of personal moments I'd captured with my Kodak Brownie.

I dealt the square, deckle-edged photos around to the writers and editors. I was particularly proud of a picture in which I'd managed to cram my father and the Washington Monument into the frame. It was only when the office staff members laughed that I realized that the monument was sprouting from my dad's head.

Walter, the managing editor, came over and saw my photos. He asked about one that showed an accident victim being rescued from an overturned car. Where did it happen? When? It was two weeks old, but he liked it so much that, in order to have an excuse to use it, he assigned a reporter to do an exposé of dangerous local parkways. Since we were short on features, it would run on the front page next week.

When I opened that issue and saw the photo I'd taken splashed across four columns, I instantly made the leap from art student to published photographer. A switch had been thrown, a connection made. Ahead was a future in which I could make pictures for profit and fame. I was very proud, and the larger-than-usual paycheck I received that week seemed like a diploma. I would have framed it if I hadn't needed it for my car payment.

The next week, Walter, apparently having promoted me, ordered me to go to the nearby town of Mount Vernon to make a photo to illustrate a story about a woman who had a collection of live birds. He plunked down a large, formidable-looking camera and a roll of film on my desk. When I said I didn't know how to use any camera other than my Brownie, he said, "Don't worry, I'll write out the instructions and you just follow 'em."

He carefully typed the camera's operating instructions and directions for lighting the photo on a single sheet of paper. At every stoplight on my drive to the woman's house, I read a bit more of Walter's crash course in picture making. I was still reading as I arrived, and I talked myself through the instructions as I set up the equipment in the living room, near the woman's many bird cages. She waited patiently for me to finish reading and fussing with the equipment. Then she placed a little parakeet on her finger. It pecked gently at her lips while she crooned, "Mommy's little Tweetie sweetie baby . . ."

As the bird lady and her bird made kissy faces at each other, I found the camera's shutter release and then the winding knob. She talked to Tweetie and I talked my way through the tutorial. I didn't feel as though I was taking pictures; what I was doing was getting to the end of Walter's instruction list. But one of the photos I took that day ran in the next issue, four columns wide at the top of page one, and for the next three days people at the paper told me that the picture was a riot. They said I was so clever to make the lady look exactly like her bird.

I was uncomfortable receiving the praise. No one seemed to know how lucky I'd been. Somehow I'd met the technical challenge, but I had nothing to do with what the woman did while I was fiddling with the gear. I hadn't intended to make her look amusing; it had simply happened.

I confessed this to Walter. I didn't want credit for something I hadn't done and, maybe more important, I didn't want him to start depending on me to do it again. I couldn't count on being lucky twice. Walter was silent for a long time before he spoke. Finally he said, "You made that bird lady picture. It didn't make itself. There was no photograph before you tripped the shutter. There was something inside you that told you when to make that photo. Just as you're responsible for making a mistake, you're also responsible for making a great picture. Moments fly by all the time; some people can sense and capture them. When you capture a moment, you're the author of what's in the photo. And if you don't believe that, it probably won't happen again. But if you do, it will happen more and more."

I appreciated that Walter was trying to reassure me, but I thought he was talking a little crazy. Somehow, though, my luck held. I made pictures, and I became passionate about making them. It was fun and it was thrilling, like telling a joke and having people laugh. A picture in a magazine could make millions of people pause, smile, feel wonder.

I discovered that there was an audience out there, and I was driven by a sense of urgency to capture images from everyday life as I saw them, and present them in ways that the audience had never expected. Look at how that inchworm glows as the sun strikes it from behind and creates a halo of light. See the rainbow colors swirl on the oil-slicked pavement. See how the town's mayor looks evil when I catch him looking sideways at the lens and the light's coming up from below.

Thirty years flew by. I became a successful freelancer and worked my way to a position where I was being copied and quoted. I had figured out the rules and regulations for success. No assignment was too tough. I could convert any miserable scene into something eye-catching. I had the bag of tricks. I had the formulas.

Then I realized that the formulas were doing the work. I was just coasting, not really paying attention to where I was headed—and where I was headed was into a loop. I began to repeat myself. New clients got the old solutions. I found myself facetiously referring to one particular lighting trick as number 22-B. I was on creative autopilot.

Then clients who wanted fresh-looking photography started asking me, "What have you done new that you can show us?" New? Why did they want new when everything was working so well?

I was busy working my way out of business. Worse, I was not having fun anymore. Trapped by my own rules and regulations, I ignored new ideas as being too chancy. No risk, no failure. But also no new stuff, no fun. The passion and joy faded away. So did many of the clients.

If I didn't find a way to inject some fun and excitement into my work, I realized, I might as well just open a Pictures-While-U-Wait passport photo shop. "Need any film or batteries today? How 'bout a lottery ticket?"

I told all this to a group of photographer friends, many of whom had bogged down too. I said I was tired of being bored doing what I used to love. Then I found myself saying that I was going to go out to shoot "just for the fun of it." I was going to "rediscover the lost excitement" that years ago had fueled my picture making.

What was I saying? Truthfully, I was pretty much just venting and posturing. But my friends called my bluff by inquiring, quite seriously, when I would be showing the first pictures from this mission.

So I decided to do it.

Flea markets, with their lure of treasures in a sea of junk, had always been a passion of mine. I would go out and shoot flea markets. No plans, no rules, no formulas, just a road trip to visit as many open-air flea markets as I could in two summer weeks.

And so I drove around the Northeast, finding flea markets and shooting whatever caught my eye: old chrome toasters reflecting puffy clouds in a pure blue sky; clusters of snow globes with Jesus and Elvis and singing pigs inside; boxes of bottle caps, marbles, campaign pins. As I walked the aisles, I began to feel stirrings I hadn't felt in years. The film was flying through the camera. The pictures came pouring out of me, the kind of pictures I'd taken years ago with my Brownie just for the love of it. The photos were funny and elegant and wonderful. I pictured patterns and played with odd juxtapositions. Seen in the orange light of sunrise, even racks of hanging gym socks or jars of pickled peppers can be visually thrilling.

I wrote daily journal entries and sent them by email to friends and colleagues who wanted to hear how the trip was going. All of a sudden, I was having fun again.

The trouble was, I didn't want it to end, and when the two weeks were over, I wanted more. I needed another mission, and it didn't take me long to realize what it should be.

For years, while on the road doing jobs, I had been noticing funny names of towns, little places I had zoomed past in rental cars while dashing to and from remote shooting locations. I remembered thinking, can you keep a straight face if you live in Goofy Ridge? How many people find Romance and then mail a letter from there? Can you buy an ice-cold bottle of Coke in Hell? Who lives in Peculiar?

I made a list from memory. With the help of a computer road-mapping program, the list grew. I found names of places that made me laugh out loud: Ding Dong, Difficult, Boring. I decided I was going to go to Surprise, Toad Suck, and Pig and make pictures of folks who lived in these charmingly named towns. And there, in the remote corners of my country, I was going to get the fun back.

I purchased maps and made phone calls to local county governments and sheriff's departments. I discovered that some of these towns, though still there officially, had been forgotten by local residents. Some, mere pin-pricks on the map, had been consumed and digested by expanding suburban ooze. But others were thriving despite the less-than-serious quality a silly name bestows.

I'd make the journey in Big Red, my trusty four-wheel-drive Trooper that I love more than a grown-up is supposed to love a car. There would be thousands of miles of driving. I would need help, with both the driving and the picture making: an assistant, someone to hold the reflectors and work the portable lights. So I called Matt Proulx, the best freelance professional photo assistant I'd ever worked with. He laughed when he heard what I was going to do, said he could use a break from the routine, and agreed to join me.

I visited my local AAA office for a face-to-face consultation. I wanted them to see that I wasn't kidding when I said I needed a map of every state in the Union. I was reassured when an overworked, beleaguered travel counselor laughed out loud when I said I would be traveling to Toad Suck.

I ordered from the DeLorme company their wonderfully detailed road atlases. Every scraggly, petered-out former road shows on their maps. Now I could get lost and find out exactly how I got there. When I put all the maps on my scale, the needle swung to sixty-five pounds.

I spent weeks studying the maps and the Internet to find the best routes between the towns I'd selected. I had narrowed the towns down from 200 to 75 by eliminating unpronounceable names, like Chassahowitzka, that didn't conjure images. Maps and guidebooks were all over my living room. I used little sticky dots to mark pages and places. One night as I was working my cat walked by with two dots from Delaware stuck to his tail.

But the biggest problem was not getting there, but finding someone to photograph when we did. I didn't want to drive hundreds of miles and not find someone to shoot, or arrive on the day when every resident—all six of them—was out of town. I made phone calls, trying to line up people at the most remote locations. It was hard work for a fast-talking New Yorker to try to explain the project to people who operated at a more leisurely pace. All the police departments, properly suspicious, declined to offer any information on the phone, but poured out details when we showed our faces.

I decided I'd done all I could in the planning department.

Ultimately, we broke the project down into bite-sized pieces. There would be several long trips taken over a period of years; that way we'd get back to our families periodically, and the two of us would be able to remain friends. Besides, after the first trip, if the pictures were lousy, I could call it a bad idea and bail out.

As I had with the flea market project, I decided to take my laptop computer to keep notes and post a daily journal to a professional photographers' Internet forum.

For all the fun we thought the project was going to be, there was some uncertainty. Would we crash and die on the turnpike (probably just after paying the toll)? Would we be robbed and killed in the middle of the night at some Bates Motel–like place? Would residents of a rural, backwoods town put two New Yorkers in jail because they asked for a toasted bagel?

Despite the risks involved in the venture, we were ready to go. We tested the camera equipment, checked out the new CB radio, and loaded the Trooper with the maps, film, cameras, model release forms, a few photographic lights, some clothing and personal supplies, and a cooler full of diet root beer and fruit juices. We said good-bye to wives and lovers and kids and cats.

It was time to go photograph the bird lady.

As we pull up to a remote general store, we see three older folks sitting on a nearby porch. One of them shouts, "Ya ain't sellin' anything, is ya? 'Cause we ain't buyin'!" Hostile town, I think. We're playing defense before we even get out of the car.

But it turns out it's all show. They're extremely friendly, and when we ask about the history of the town's name, we're told to go inside the store and talk with "ol' J. C. Pickett, who knows everything."

Inside we find J. C., who is so eager to help that he follows us around until I have to ask him to sit down while I scout for a good spot to take his picture. While I look around I ask him about the town's name. He says that Sweetlips is called such because two Civil War soldiers, who were surveying and making maps, stopped at a local stream on a scorching summer day and drank water they described as "tasting sweet to the lips." They labeled the spot on their map Sweetlips.

J. C. shows us the edge of town a half-mile up the road. It's marked by a homemade sign that's nailed to a tree up a steep embankment. Fearful of the rugged terrain, I do my looking from the road, but J. C., twenty-five years my senior, bolts straight up the hill through the rough brush to show me the sign.

As he poses for us, J. C. is part Popeye, part country curmudgeon. Of the cigarette clamped between his lips, he says, "Doc tells me to quit, but I ain't never gonna. I had two strokes and an aneurysm and I'm still kickin'."

He has a nice smile when it appears, and he doesn't want to stop posing, but we have to be on our way.

SWEETLIPS
Tennessee
J. C. Pickett, surveyor, construction worker

N othing sits in the middle of nowhere. Its informal address is the 148 $^1/_2$ mile marker on Route 60. We pull in and greet Richard Kenworthy, the town's owner and one-fourth of its population. He smiles and gives us the history in a few sentences: "I picked this place for myself and three other drunks a bunch of years ago. When I told one of them about the property I'd bought, he said, 'It sounds like nothing to me. You oughta call it Nothing.' So I did."

Richard runs a small garage and store where he sits with his ring-eyed mutt, Katy, who looks like a junkyard dog but turns out to be OK. Richard's been working hard at merchandising this four-person town: the little shack that houses the store is crammed with Nothing stuff. There are Nothing T-shirts, Nothing postcards, Nothing hats. Matt and I have been collecting souvenir mugs from the towns we've visited but, unfortunately, there are no Nothing mugs available.

Richard says that he and one of the other residents have been sober for a number of years now, and they live down close to the road where the business is. The other two, he says, are still drunk, and the sober ones keep them living at the back of the property—"to keep them away from the road with the traffic and all." I think, traffic?

It's 6:30 P.M. and clouds have rolled in. About to lose daylight, we talk fast and shoot faster. When it begins to snow we have a perfect excuse to buy caps that read "Tain't Much. Nothing, Arizona, Pop. 4."

NOTHING
Arizona
Richard Kenworthy, owner

Three hours north out of New York City we reach the edge of the Catskill Mountains and sail into a state trooper barracks near the town of Surprise to ask where the town really is and inquire about finding volunteers to be photographed.

The desk dispatcher takes a call, listens, puts the phone down, and explains that the town has pretty much gone away with the closing of the post office years back. All he knows of the town today is a little green state sign reading, simply, "Surprise." He smiles as he says this, and I know we've hooked someone who will help us.

He listens to our story about how we're "doing a book and visiting some U.S. towns with unique names," yadda yadda. I ask if he knows any troopers who might want to pose next to the sign. He thinks for a moment, looks over his shoulder to see who's in the barracks behind him, and then slowly raises his finger and dials the phone. Matt and I take this as a good sign; he's thought of someone and is dialing him up.

We wait, confident that we are about to score a good model for our picture. But when the dispatcher speaks into the phone, he says, "Unit 32, there's a burglar alarm sounding at Quarry Hardware. Please check it out."

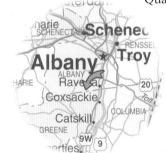

Geez! He listens to us for a good five minutes after taking an alarm call and *then* dispatches a unit to the site? Who'd have imagined photographers would be that important?

Soon a uniformed officer named Paul Hogan (yes, they call him Crocodile Dundee) is dispatched in his police car to pose for us. We can only assume there's no police business for him to attend to.

We find the Surprise sign and meet up with Trooper Hogan, who refuses to show anything but his best serious cop face to the camera. We don't care and shoot him just that way, with a little bit of Surprise showing in the background.

He has fun and so do we. We shoot for about an hour until the mosquitoes come out at twilight and the flash's batteries die.

SURPRISE

New York

Paul Hogan, state trooper

n case you've ever wondered, Purgatory is not a bad place to spend a little time. It's a cluster of houses on a bend in the road between Bachelors Crossing and Litchfield in lovely central Maine where the tiny Country Cafe serves up the biggest and best fresh lobster roll I've ever had.

It's a clear, Sunday morning, and we're checking things out at the church, trying to see if we can identify our subject, eighty-four-year-old Helen Allen, among the hugging and hand-shaking parishioners leaving the service. We've arranged to meet her at her home, and we've already location-scouted her house, but we're trying to get an advance look at who we'll be shooting.

We study the crowd and realize that nobody dresses up for church around here. Shorts, sportswear, and other casual clothing hallmark this crowd. The only person wearing Sunday clothes is an older lady in a long pink dress. "Helen!" we proclaim. But then the pink lady gets into a car that heads away from Helen's house.

We drive to Helen's house. Her car is there. We spied on the wrong congregation.

Helen, a jaunty woman who looks ten years younger than her age, tells us that Purgatory got its name when Governor Gardiner went fishing on the outskirts of Litchfield during the region's infamous blackfly season. The fishing was good, but the flies were voracious. When the governor returned home, his wife almost fainted at the sight of the lumpy red welts all over his body. "Where on earth have you been?" she screamed. His reply was, "I've been fishing. Fishing in Purgatory."

Helen was a letter carrier for years before she became the town's postmaster. "Driving those mail routes was the best because people would bring food to you at the mailbox and sit and talk," she says. "The food was great. I might not have taken the postmaster's job if I knew I was going to miss that food so much."

Helen has two pitchforks we can use as props. She likes the idea of holding a pitchfork because she says that when she was a little girl there was actually a pitchfork mill in Purgatory.

We set up at high noon right in the middle of the world's ugliest sunlight. I position her in the shade of the big oak on her front lawn. With light from our reflector on Helen's face we get a nice effect. I use the clouds as a background. The pitchfork looks out of place and a little disturbing. Perfect.

We try a few other locations before the blackflies arrive on the scene.

PURGATORY

Maine

Helen Allen, retired postmaster

The hardwood trees are tinged with the orange and red of early fall as we sail into the hill country of West Virginia. We've filled the gas tank three times in order to get here from New York City.

We meet the principal of the Left Hand Elementary School, who tells us he thinks the town got its name because it sits on the left hand fork of a creek. He suggests his secretary, Billie Taylor, as our portrait subject, and we photograph her in the hallway against a background of orange lockers and a poster of tiny handprints. She tells us that all twenty first-graders pressed their painted left hands onto the poster paper. It's perfect for our picture.

She works very hard at posing for us, following our every request to the letter. She is extremely focused on what she's doing, and when a passing fifth-grader pauses to watch us work, she doesn't take her eyes from the lens as she snaps from the corner of her mouth, "Are you where you're supposed to be, young man?" The kid literally runs off to his class-room. Grown men, Matt and I are once again awed by the power of a truly great school administrator.

LEFT HAND
West Virginia
Kathryn "Billie" Taylor, school secretary

The early-morning light is sweet and perfect as we roll up to Bonnie's Corner Cafe in Gas. Inside we see platters of food and plates of loose sunny-side-up eggs alongside piles of bacon glistening with grease. I also see the traditional biscuits-'n'-gravy meal: pale flour biscuits drowning in a white gravy that except for its mysterious lumps resembles watery tile grout.

Bonnie, helpful and a good sport about our project, agrees to pose outside, offering a platter of food to the camera—and I mean right *into* the camera. I use a 20mm wide-angle lens for that '50s TV-commercial look. I can hear the announcer's voice as I shoot: "And here's how a *real* plow jockey starts his day!"

We shoot many rolls in an amazingly short time, with Bonnie holding the plate so that the sun hitting from behind makes the food look even shinier than it is.

She's not sure of the origin of the town's name, but we've been told that in the area there once were two petroleum refining plants a few miles apart. In between was a collection of buildings used for the processing and storage of the natural gas by-product of the refining, and the little cluster of buildings comprising the natural-gas plant was referred to by the workers simply as Gas.

I ask Bonnie if people make fun of the name of her town. She says, "Well, when people ask us how to find the town, we tell them to come on down the highway, and then we tell them that if they blink, they're gonna pass Gas!" We all laugh so hard that for several minutes no photos are shot.

When I hint at the possible relationship between the name of the town and her establishment, she smiles as if she has never before considered such a connection.

As we leave I'm thinking that you've got to be a pretty darn good cook to run a thriving lunchroom in Gas.

GAS
Kansas
Bonnie Steward, owner, Bonnie's Corner Cafe

Crapo is five or six houses and a post office, and it sits just outside a bird reserve on land that's as sparsely populated as any part of the country we've visited, except maybe Montana and North Dakota. Driving through the area we can smell the salt from the marshes, and we see lots of wild waterfowl that to us city boys seem pretty exotic. We also see what looks like an eagle.

Crapo is, of course, pronounced *cray-po*, and it comes from someone's family name. And sure, every out-of-towner mispronounces it, but the locals don't seem to mind.

As we drive in, the late-afternoon sky is overcast. I think I've got some kind of flu; I'm groggy and feverish.

We find Larry Bennett, a commercial crab and oyster fisherman who's working on his house. We ask him to pose for us outside the post office. He says, "Sure," and then adds, "my mom is the postmaster."

He brings his two little girls, Courtney and Danielle, and we start what can only be described as a panic shoot: quick composition with film and filters adjusted for the awful gray light. It's becoming nighttime fast, nothing much is happening, I'm sick, and we're definitely up against a wall here.

The two girls are lurking off-camera, and we ask them if they want to be in the picture. They have no interest. Larry tries to bribe them with ice cream—after the shoot, but before their mom comes home—but they aren't having any of it. I know they can help save the picture. They've been lurking alongside the cab of the pickup Larry's leaning on; now they're on the roof of the cab. We subtly move Larry over so the 20mm wide-angle lens gets him, the post office sign, and the girls in the frame. Matt starts making faces at the girls; they respond by sticking out their tongues. The picture finally works.

As we're packing up, I compliment Matt on his child-wrangling skills.

CRAPO
Maryland
Larry Bennett, fisherman, and his daughters, Courtney and Danielle

We leave the interstate and begin a plunge deep into the lush green of central Pennsylvania farmland. This is nontourist, rural farming country, which has hills like those in Vermont except that the roads don't switch back and forth, they just climb up and over. We follow a pickup truck with two farmers aboard. The driver takes the state's speed suggestions literally, so we climb hills at thirty miles per hour and descend at thirty-five. There is no possibility of passing because the roads are so narrow, steep, and winding. The driver ahead has no idea that a foaming-at-the-mouth New Yorker is using terrible language in a futile effort to get him to go faster so we can see the town of Rough and Ready before nightfall. Every time I suggest tooting my horn at him, Matt whistles the opening bars of "Dueling Banjos."

Finally we get to Rough and Ready and find that it's just a church and a few houses. We stop in a driveway to look at a vista for a possible shoot and a woman comes out to see what's going on. We explain what we're doing.

Immediately grasping the concept, she starts laughing at the idea of shooting portraits of locals in towns with funny names and suggests that her sixteen-year-old daughter would be perfect for the shoot.

We do a quick scout, find two good locations, and ask Valerie, her daughter, to bring her bike as a lean-against prop. Valerie tells us that two miles over the ridge is the town of Fearnot, and that her dad saved a local newspaper clipping from the '30s with the headline "Fearnot Man Marries Rough and Ready Woman." We shoot two settings. Everything looks good.

ROUGH AND READY

Pennsylvania

Valerie Troutman, student

Driving the unbelievably beautiful back roads of the Susquehanna River Valley, we make heartfelt, touristy "ooh" and "ahh" exclamations. We roll up and down glens and see pastoral landscapes that look like they were drawn by Disney artists.

We're about a mile from Fearnot when we come over the crest of a hill and see a man leap out of a pickup truck parked on the grass. He's brandishing a stop sign on a stick, and he faces it in our direction. He wants to be sure we don't run afoul of his partner, who is riding the county weed-whacker and brush-chomper to keep rogue grasses from devouring the already narrow road. When the chomper is clear of the road, he waves us on. As we pass, we see he's a very imposing, slightly scary-looking fellow. We stop to see if we can make small talk with him about Fearnot.

His name is Chris Morgan, and he says his brother, Gregg, lives on a farm about a half-mile up the road. He asks if we would be interested in seeing the cemetery that he and his brother found in a stand of trees on the property. For some reason I'm positively gleeful at the prospect of shooting in a cemetery, but when we get there it's a disappointment. There is only one sizable headstone inscribed with an illegible name and the date 1793 and two or three pet-sized stones scattered around.

Instead, we go into a tall stand of corn and photograph the brothers, who stand holding their hunting shotguns, looking for all the world like guys you would not ever want to mess with.

The Morgans don't know how Fearnot got its name. The original name of the town was Spread Eagle, apparently of Indian origin. Later it was called Cressona. When an official name was needed for the post office, Cressona was offered, but it turned out there was another Cressona just a few miles down the road. So the town became Fearnot, in a reference to the Bible, or so the brothers think. They are very nice fellows despite our efforts to make them look sinister in the portrait.

We have a wonderful time swapping stories. When I mention that I photographed a teenager named Valerie Troutman in the town of Rough and Ready, about two miles away on the other side of the ridge, Chris says, "I went to school with her."

As we drive away I say to Matt, "Isn't it amazing? Coming back here and finding a person who went to school with Valerie?" Matt says, "What's so amazing? There can't be more than one school here for the whole county."

He's right. I'm still a city boy, wandering the heartland, agog at almost everything.

FEARNOT

Pennsylvania
Chris and Gregg Morgan, brothers

We reach Zip City without having made any arrangements for a portrait subject. It's almost five in the afternoon, late to start prospecting, but we try a diner–general store. The owner's manner is as ugly as the greenish glow from the fluorescent bulbs that light the interior. He tries hard not to understand what we're taking about. He's unlike the cordial majority we've met so far, so we chalk it up to his desire to get us out of there so he can close up shop for the day.

We spot a small flea-market auction starting up across the street. The lot is filled with pickups loaded with fence gates, farm implements, and other treasures. The lot is also filled with good ol' boys, each one in a form-fitting, polyester striped shirt or a black T-shirt emblazoned with brightly colored logos representing everything from beer to local AM radio stations. Most of the shirts look like they were sized for slimmer people. I wonder why people without much form wear such form-fitting clothes.

The people are friendly and helpful, but no one seems to know how Zip City got its name. We're told that the Keetons, owners of the P&K Western Store, are the oldest businesspeople in town and they should know.

Early the next morning we pull up to the P&K to find the door open. Barbara Keeton, her rat-faced dog, CoCo, and her orange tabby, Charlie, greet us. She says that Zip City is rumored to have gotten its name in the days of Prohibition, when cars would drive slowly through town on their way to speakeasies and, later in the night when everyone was boozed, zoom back through at high speed. As the story goes, Lonzo Parker, the general store owner at that time, said, "The way they drive through here, we oughta name this place Zip City." And they did.

Barbara is thrilled to pose, but she worries about her hair. She brings Charlie outside at my request and poses next to the arrow sign pointing from the driveway toward the store. Charlie, the friendliest store cat I've ever met, looks in control, as cats do, until the camera's shutter fires. For some reason, he hates the shutter's sound and flings himself to the pavement. Maybe he's a veteran of cat food advertising shoots and associates the camera's sound with yet another miserable mouthful of some awful kitty chow.

ZIP CITY
Alabama
Barbara Keeton, store owner, and CoCo

Boogertown yields a young, relaxed, well-to-do-couple who have a good time posing in the rain under a colorful, photogenic umbrella at a muddy construction site on the crest of Booger Mountain.

We're first told that Boogertown's name comes from a racial slur used to describe poor black workers who lived here over a century ago. Then a Booger Mountain developer eagerly jumps into the conversation to "straighten out the story." He says the name comes from the mispronunciation of Boger (he pronounces it *Boó-jair*), the name of a notorious local fugitive Frenchman. I don't know if I'm buying this, especially when I notice that his explanation is greeted by a rolling of eyes and an arching of brows by David and Leslie.

As we hose red clay from our shoes, Matt and I wonder about the difficulty of selling homes on Booger Mountain.

BOOGERTOWN

North Carolina

David and Leslie Cline, business owners

To get directions to Embarrass, we call our subject, Terry Newman, a Pentecostal minister who preaches at the newly reborn nondenominational Church of Embarrass. On the phone he is at once extremely cheerful and slightly leery. I apply my best fatherly tone to assure him that we are going to make appropriately serious photographs. Satisfied, he gives detailed lefts and rights.

The church is a mile and a half off a farm road in one of those clusters of trees that provide farmers with their only shelter from the blazing, crop-growing sun. At the location is a hundred-year-old cemetery. There's also a small family park with playground swings so you can picnic with the perished. Here a Sunday with the family can include several generations, even some family members no longer among the living.

A wonderful wrought-iron arch with "Embarrass Cemetery" written in bent-iron script will be a perfect frame for the picture. The arch will flow over the minister's head, black against the sky, with the fields of tall corn stalks filling the background to the horizon.

Terry Newman turns out to be close to three hundred pounds of charming, jovial, utterly engaging minister. He shows me the spot in the chapel, near the organ, where he recently removed a twenty-foot tall, floor-to-ceiling wasp nest.

Both he and his soon-to-be-ordained wife love the picture idea. Their constant laughter and jolly mood is infectious, and for the rest of the day Matt and I are uncharacteristically courteous to the offensive drivers we encounter, calling each and every one Mr. Jerk or Ms. Moron.

EMBARRASS

Illinois

Terry Newman, minister, Church of Embarrass

After doing calculations to figure out where the rising sun will strike the front of the tiny post office in Romance, Arkansas, we arrive to find that for the first time during our various trips we are absolutely correct. The sun is casting a sideways glow on the front of the building, and it looks like it's going to last for another fifteen or twenty minutes. We dash inside and find Lynda, the postmaster, sorting mail. There are hurried introductions, during which I grind my teeth impatiently—I want her to postpone the mail sorting because we have great light right now. On the outside I'm smiling, while inside I'm screaming: If you don't stop chatting with the customers and finish that sorting I'll go postal! But I repress the thought and politely explain that we're losing some really pretty light. I should have said it sooner. Lynda happily ceases her sorting and we go shooting.

It turns out Lynda's not only hard working, she's resourceful too. The U.S. Postal Service had intended to close her post office because it served a community that consisted of only four farming families. Lynda fought back by advertising in bride's magazines that she would hand-cancel all wedding invitations with the official stamp of Romance if readers would send her their boxes of wedding invitations along with a check to cover the postage. Currently Lynda's doing more than half a million invitations a year and the post office is actually making money.

How did the town get its name in the first place? From Romance Creek, so named because it was the local lovers' lane.

ROMANCE
Arkansas
Lynda Pickard, postmaster

Peculiar got its name due to a misunderstanding. In the early part of the twentieth century, when the post office asked the town to supply a name for the mail district, three successive choices were rejected because they were already in use. The town fathers, who had better things to do, sent a message saying that they didn't care what the name was, and that the post office could pick any name it wanted as long as it was peculiar—meaning, in the language of the day, unique. Well, they got what they wanted: a unique name.

We arrive in town in the late afternoon and scout our location for the next day's shoot. Our subject, Becky Klein, a teacher at the Peculiar Elementary School, has told us that Peculiarites like to talk about their unique three-legged water tower. We figure that it's a good picture possibility, but when we get to the tower we see that someone has placed a small satellite dish on its railing, so the town's name on the tower reads "Pec" and "iar." So much for that location.

We drive a mile into the countryside but find no great "Peculiar" signs. I decide to head back. As I'm making a U-turn I spot a red plastic pinwheel planted in the grass at the side of the road, spinning in the setting sun. Between the pinwheel and the pavement are four hearts fashioned of thin red metal. We drive up slowly and see that it's a

shrine. There is a six-foot-high, handmade sign that displays photographs of four young women, three of whom appear to be teenage sisters. The sign reads, "Four lives lost because of a careless driver." There is a palpable sense of grief and despair here. For three or four minutes we don't move or speak. I stare at the shrine and try to imagine the loss felt by those who built it. There is no way I can. I don't take a picture.

The next day, in 97-degree midday heat, we make pictures of Becky standing by a highway sign that points the way to the town. I usually like to work the heck out of a scene, shooting as many as seven or eight rolls of film in thirty minutes, but this day is so unbelievably hot and oppressive that all we can manage is fifteen minutes of shooting.

PECULIAR
Missouri
Becky Klein, teacher

On the way to Looneyville we stop to talk with three men who are on, in, and under an old pickup truck at the road's edge. I ask if this is Looneyville and I'm told it is. Then I ask if anyone knows how Looneyville got to be Looneyville. From under the hood we hear: "Lived here all my life, and I don't have any idea." From the truck cab: "Tell him to ask John." From under the truck: "Right, you should ask ol' John Belknap. He's been here over seventy years." It seems that ol' John is the town's elder and knows everything about things in Looneyville. I'm told we're likely to find him riding his bicycle about a mile up the road.

We stumble on John, who is more listener than talker, but he likes the idea of having his picture taken. So does a neighbor kid, Justin, who bikes circles around the old man while Matt and I set up to take John's photo in a sliver of disappearing sunlight. We figure that the best way to keep Justin under control is to put him in the picture, so we set him in the background as we pose John astride the new two-wheeler he's just bought for himself. We fire off five rolls as the sun pinches itself off behind a ridge.

John tells us that the town got its name from a family named Looney who, in the late 1700s, settled in the area. When we ask him if folks are ever uncomfortable with the other meaning, he smiles and says, "Naw, we got some folks here that pretty much live up to the name."

LOONEYVILLE

West Virginia

John Belknap, retired factory worker

When we arrive in Tightwad we find Tom, a volunteer fireman as well as the town's mayor. We decide we want to photograph him at 6:00 p.m., when the lower sun will provide better light, in front of the barn-like fire station. Tom agrees to meet us then. I ask him to be sure to wear his fireman's turnout coat and hat.

At 6:00 the light is at a good angle, and we shoot a lot of film of Tom before it starts to look like the weight of his coat and the late afternoon heat might be a dangerous the combination for him.

We learn the town's name comes from a century-old incident in which a local store owner accepted a customer's deposit for an item, then sold the item to a higher bidder. The jilted customer shouted at the store owner, "You damn tightwad, I'll never shop here again!" Soon after the incident the store became known as Tightwad's. Later, when the local post office, which was located inside the store, became official, the town needed a name and the store's designation was passed on.

Tightwad has a population of only forty-three people (Tom admits that it wasn't hard to become mayor) but there is a bank and we're told to go there to mail our postcards. Inside the bank's front door is a mailbox. The problem is, a month ago some-

one robbed the bank and they no longer leave the door open for mail drops. We have to use the drive-up window to deposit our cards.

Tom says he thinks this is the most-robbed bank in the state. He thinks some robbers just want to claim the bank of Tightwad among their scores. We ponder the concept of whimsical bank robbers. Tom smiles at the thought that someone would stick up the bank in daylight hours. He says, "Heck, the bank is a house trailer. They could just show up at night, hook up, and drive off with the whole thing."

We leave town wondering what kind of losers would rob the Bank of Tightwad.

TIGHTWAD
Missouri
Tom Skaggs, mayor and firefighter

Picture Perfect

This book is the result of nine separate journeys from my home in New York, journeys made over a five-year period as I pursued my quest to visit strangely-named towns and make a portrait of a resident in each one.

Just finding the town was sometimes a problem; finding a subject was often a difficult task. Making the picture, however, was the greatest challenge. Photography is all about light, and we were always chasing it, fighting to control it, and bemoaning its fleeting nature.

As I look back on my notes, these are the phrases that leap out at me:

"Things don't look good for photography today . . ."

"There's a sodden, falling mist that resembles coarse fog . . ."

"I have no sun and no lighting equipment . . ."

Once, on a weekend trip, in a desperate attempt to combat poor light, I dashed into an Office Max, bought three poster-size Foamcore boards and a can of spray adhesive. Then at a paint store I bought a can of gold spray paint

and at a supermarket a roll of aluminum foil. I sprayed the Foamcore boards with adhesive and laid a covering of foil on each one. Then I lightly sprayed two of them with gold paint. Now I was in business! I had three shiny reflectors, two with a warm golden glow that would rescue any subject's skin tones from the effects of dreary, overcast gray skies.

Several times I drove all day haunted by the colorful sunrise I'd seen that morning, convinced that I was heading into a storm that would preclude any picture taking. "Red sky at morning, photographer take warning"—that's the way it goes, right?

I know, you're wondering what all the fuss is about. Just point the camera and click. After all, hasn't the photo industry named a whole class of cameras "point-and-shoot"? How hard can it be?

Well, contrary to the camera marketers' message that it's easy to capture the essence of a person or a place by just pointing and shooting, thirty years of professional photography have taught me that a good portrait is one of the hardest things to make. Capturing an engaging, casual-looking moment on film takes a little luck and a whole lot of planning. Selecting the location, figuring out how to position your subject, choosing some props and placing them well, and handling the camera with skill and dexterity all have to combine with a touch of serendipity.

The light that pro shooters are often chasing and trying to capture in the frame is light that makes its appearance during the golden hours of early morning and late afternoon. The light is low on the horizon then, extra warm in color and very flattering for people and places that are not otherwise beautiful.

But this golden light doesn't hang around. It lasts no more than an hour at each end of the day. So we scramble to set up and shoot while the light's right.

Our overall plan for the trips was to spend the bad-light time of midday driving so we'd arrive at our target town with enough time to scout, find a photo subject, and then shoot in the golden afternoon light. If that didn't work, we'd try to round up a volunteer for a morning shot.

In addition to light is the issue of location. Portrait shooting often depends on taking the best a location has to offer, and photographers need time to find the best angle and figure out what the scene will look like in good light. Many photographers actually carry a compass to determine just where the light will hit when the sun rises and sets.

What made it all tougher was the fact that we were photographing total strangers, volunteer subjects who we knew would get fidgety and begin to regret their cooperation in the project if we spent a lot of time fussing with the light and the background. That's why we did all the scouting of locations ahead of time and rushed to get things set up while we had the light. We knew it was best to find someone, explain the project, ask them to pose, and go right to the preselected location and start shooting.

Of course we carried some portable lights for indoor shots, but setting up indoor lighting takes time and nonprofessional models get antsy after fifteen minutes.

Most of the time we found the light we needed, and only once did a town fail to yield a location. That town was Hustler, Wisconsin. We drove the quiet, neat streets of this small hamlet until my hair hurt. We found nothing—nothing unusual, nothing exciting, nothing boring. It was average in every respect. Maybe we were too tired, but we never got Hustler to speak to us and suggest a picture, and so we remember it as the only town in which we just gave up and went to dinner. To this day I believe that making a portrait in Hustler would have taken the skills not of a photographer, but of an alchemist.

W drive to Nice through the lush, smooth, rolling hills of California's Sonoma Valley. A couple of veteran road warriors, we're moved to saying things like, "Oooh, look at that," and "Geez, that's pretty," and "Oh, man, it's just like a calendar."

Our reception in Nice is anything but. The owner of a local grocery store greets us with hostility. From behind the meat counter he stares blankly and angrily. His face is saying "Get the hell outta here!" We do, referring to him as "the Meat Nazi."

This tiny lakeside town has a local Harley shop called The Hog Pen. Since it's Saturday morning, all the wanna-be-bad-boy bikers turn out in their leathers to buy parts, talk shop, and hang out with the real McCoys.

We meet the Pen's owner, Rodney Harper, an ample-stomached, black-T-shirted biker with an exploding beard and a head of disheveled gray hair. His ferocious look is offset by his good-natured disposition and kind eyes. We also meet Katy, Rod's wife, who handles the register behind the parts counter. "Nice is pronounced *Neece* by some people," says Katy, rolling her eyes.

She tells us about the night that their town was mentioned by Jay Leno on *The Tonight Show*. During one of his "Headlines" segments, Jay read from the

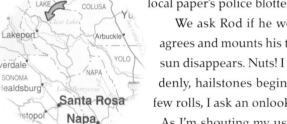

local paper's police blotter: "Nice man arrested for beating wife."

We ask Rod if he would pose on his banana-yellow trike bike. He agrees and mounts his three-wheeled hog. We begin shooting just as the sun disappears. Nuts! I wanted the sun to backlight his unruly hair. Suddenly, hailstones begin to bounce off the camera. Determined to get a few rolls, I ask an onlooker to hold the rain umbrella.

As I'm shouting my usual model encouragements to Rod, I ask him to put his elbow on the handlebar of the bike. Then, worrying that it might be an awkward position for him, I ask, "Is that comfy?" The man holding the umbrella whispers, "You might think about taking the word 'comfy' out of your vocabulary when you're talking to bikers."

We manage to get off six rolls using a reflector to help throw some light into all that hair before all hail breaks loose.

NICE

California

Rodney Harper, owner, The Hog Pen motorcycle shop

Deep in farm country we find Screamer, a crossroads of scattered houses dominated by a massive, modern brick church. We arrive in a drizzle that prohibits outdoor shooting.

Our subject is Shirley Ross, wife of the reverend, Gerald Ross, and my idea is to pose her as a choir singer hitting the high notes (I know, no points for originality here). She is a pleasant-looking woman with a sweet smile. She agrees to wear a colorful choir robe. The reverend is a forceful person who's not excited about what we're trying to do. He's more interested in talking than in listening to any idea about the photograph. His wife's obvious enjoyment forces him to comply, but not really cooperate.

Neither the reverend nor his wife is quite sure how Screamer got its name. One local story says that the nearby river once had barge traffic, and when the barges passed a local point of interest, the sailors would scream to get the attention of townspeople ashore. Another tale has it that the area was the favorite attack spot for hostile Indians, and that their screaming war cries were the reason for the name. Everyone's a bit skeptical about that one.

In response to my request, Shirley sings. She has a very pretty but very tiny voice. Her facial expressions are almost undetectable and consist of little more than breathing. I was hoping for a open-mouthed, toothy look that could conceivably resemble a scream. What I need is a full-throated gospel singer.

The reverend, who says I should call him "Brother," watches from a seat up on the preaching platform. His presence stifles any attempt to loosen up Shirley. The light is poor, and I'm sure I'm losing half my pictures to motion. I can't find a drop-dead composition to carry the subject. The reverend is making "Aren't you finished yet?" faces. Outside the rain is coming down harder and inside my subject is starting to sweat. This shot is going into the dumper.

Many photographers secretly believe in a kind of photographic divine intervention—that it's always possible that a seemingly dreary shot will come to life in one fleeting frame, maybe the frame he didn't even realize he got. Me, I've been at this game long enough to know when the shoot gods are having drinks at the nineteenth hole and I'm out there on my own.

SCREAMER
Alabama
Shirley Ross, choir member

For all its old-time country charm, Dry Run seems to be a town dying of old age. It's well off the highway, nestled behind a small hill in a farming valley. As we pull into town we see an Amish farmer, standing on his plow, raising a plume of dust as he's pulled at a snail's pace through dry dirt by a team of eight giant draft horses.

We stop at five or six houses and at the post office to ask if anybody knows how Dry Run got its name. No one has an answer. Everyone seems to be over eighty, and half admit that their memories are not so good anymore. We go to the town's retirement home and ask the administrator if any resident might know a little of the local history. She says they are all either too old to remember or suffering from Alzheimer's. It seems that we speak to almost everyone in town. Nobody knows the history and nobody wants to pose. We're coming up dry in Dry Run.

We're ready to call it quits when we pass a house and see an old gent on his porch, his leg propped up on the railing. The scene looks great and I go for it. He's Claire Hockenberry, and it turns out he's not just relaxing, but is resting his leg in the only comfortable position he can find because of pain from an injury. "I'm just messed up all through here," he explains, pointing to his groin area. He doesn't know anything about the history of the town, but his smile and posture are engaging, and I shoot him and Molly, his little pug-faced dog, simply because that little voice inside me says, "Do it, dummy."

DRY RUN

Pennsylvania

Claire Hockenberry, farmer, and Molly

The air smells of corn as we push along on a gray Saturday morning to find Goofy Ridge, which is fifty miles into nowhere. At the crossroads that is the town there's a tavern with a pickup parked in front. Inside there are four or five people sitting at the bar—a surprise given the single vehicle outside.

Our experience tells us that these first few seconds can determine how things will go. Enter too brashly and people will ignore you. Be too timid and they'll toy with you. We aim for the line right down the center, one that requires being friendly but definitely on a mission.

We ask for our contact, "Flakey" Jake Richards, the bar's owner. Immediately we're met with a series of friendly catcalls. These people knew we were coming, and they've been waiting to check us out. I greet Jake and show him some of the pictures from the project. He's impressed, and an unspoken message seems to pass to all the people inside.

Before I can ask, I get the story of how Goofy Ridge got its name—or at least the story with the widest appeal. Years back it was just The Ridge, a camp near the river bank where moonshiners and other carousers met weekly to do their drinking, compare mash, and generally have a good time. After some serious drinking one night, a local game warden said he wasn't too drunk to shoot a walnut off the head of a volunteer. Naturally, someone was drunk enough to volunteer. The game warden, whose name was Johnny Darling, placed the tiny target on the volunteer's head, aimed his .22 rifle, and shot the nut right off. The story goes that both men were so drunk they were swaying back and forth, and that Darling waited until the swaying was in synch before firing. This caper was called by a witness "one damned goofy thing to do," and the camp was ever after known as Goofy Ridge.

The folks in the bar are as friendly as can be, but they don't want to have the place made fun of because in the past so many writers have played up the lowlife aspect of its history. I point out that my photos are of nice, regular folk; the names of the towns provide the humor, not the people. I ask, "Who wants to be in a picture?" All hands go up.

I decide to shoot Jake and two of his pals outside at the crossroads. I stand on the ladder and push a 20mm wide-angle lens into the faces of the three men, who hold beer and soda cans and stand in a tight group. I say, "OK, now I need some really happy faces, big smiles, lemme see lots of teeth!" Ron, the man on the right, says, "Well, that's gonna be kinda tough. Mine are home in a glass."

I make a mental note to do a tooth check before using that line again.

GOOFY RIDGE

Illinois

Don Schmick, "Flakey" Jake Richards, and Ron Simpson, bar buddies

The only building in sight at the tiny bridge crossing where the Toad Suck Ferry used to be is Ozzie's Toad Suck One Stop convenience store.

Ozzie is amenable to anything we want to do, but he's got to take care of his customers because his assistant hasn't come in yet. We do a quick scout for angles that will show Ozzie's sign, but with the rain falling and the generally miserable look of the site, I can't find a satisfying view. Every few minutes someone stops in to get a few gallons of gas or have a chicken sandwich made, and Ozzie has to dart inside to attend to business. Despite the fact that there isn't any other local place for these folks to get their gas or chicken sandwiches, Ozzie is determined to take care of his customers without delay.

The rain slows to a drizzle and we dash outside and do a quick setup in which Ozzie leans on his ice freezer and we come in close with a wide-angle lens to show his sign and the gas pumps.

The customers keep coming. Ozzie remarks that he's never been this busy before noon. Because of the rain, the brisk business Ozzie is doing, the customers trying to drive their pickups into our setup, and my inability to think of a decent picture, I shoot lots of film— Ozzie smiling, Ozzie with his hat on, Ozzie with his hat off—all of it between his making sandwiches and ringing up gas sales.

Ozzie tells us that Toad Suck got its name from the old ferry boat captains who on hot days would sit on deck between crossings "and suck down moonshine whiskey 'til they swole up like toads." On really hot afternoons, he says, locals would avoid the crossing because they feared disaster at the hands of incapacitated captains.

We drive away with two Toad Suck coffee mugs.

TOAD SUCK
Arkansas
Ozzie Aslakson, owner, Ozzie's Toad Suck One Stop

When we stop at the general store and ask about Intercourse, the response is a blizzard of wisecracks and funny stories. Nancy—a self-proclaimed "damn Yankee, just like you guys"—tells us that Intercourse got its name when locals starting calling the crossroads where the general store sits "the Intercourse."

Many years ago the townspeople noticed that for such a small place in the middle of nowhere they were having a lot of auto accidents. Cars were inexplicably crashing into a giant tree a few yards from the general store. The accidents remained a mystery until one day a survivor of the most recent crash mentioned that he was trying to re-read a sign he had just passed outside what was the town's meeting hall. The sign stated, "Intercourse Lessons Wednesday Night." It referred to sewing instruction, but the drivers' double-takes were causing them to crash into the tree. The sign came down and the accident rate dropped right away.

We pose Nancy at one of the oak trees that stands at the site of the long-gone building and the notorious sign. We shoot her laughing into the camera as the sun sets behind her.

INTERCOURSE
Alabama
Nancy B. Ezell, widow

We drive into a wilderness atop a shallow ridge looking for a sign to tell us that we have, indeed, found the town of Scratch Ankle. Folks just ten miles back said they'd never heard of it. With about ten minutes of daylight left, we see a man walk out of his house and get into a pickup truck. I zoom the Trooper up to his driveway, block his exit and muster my best "I'm lost" expression. I ask if we are near Scratch Ankle, and he smiles and says, "This is it." He asks what we're looking for and I explain in one sentence that we need to find a person to photograph for a book project. He grins, pops the door open and bounds out of the truck. And—my God!—he's not wearing any shoes or socks. Bare ankles! When I ask him if he'd be willing to be in our photograph, he lights up like a thousand-watt bulb. "Oh, boy," he says. "You've just made my year!" He tells us his name is Chris McKinley and we agree to meet at eight the next morning.

We arrive at Chris's house on time after a sluggish drive behind slow-moving farm pickups and I'm-in-no-hurry locals in family sedans, one of whom was swerving all over the road on four temporary doughnut spares.

It strikes us that this ankle thing is more than just a funny name. Scratch Ankle is a barefoot bastion: Chris greeted us in his bare feet the night before, and many folks were walking around the Piggly Wiggly market barefooted this morning. Something's up here.

Chris's dad tells us that the town got its name from the folks in the next town, who used to ride their carriages to church on Sunday. When they passed the residents of this hill, where the mosquito swarms were thick, they saw that the locals were always scratching their ankles as they sat on their porches. So the area was referred to as Scratch Ankle.

The sun is coursing across his lawn as Chris, once again shoeless, trots across the wet grass to greet us. We ask him to sit up on the edge of the cargo bed of an old red pickup truck parked nearby. He leaps up, gives us a friendly grin and steadies himself by resting his bare foot on the door handle. This can't be an easy pose to hold, but he's determined to help us and manages to tough it out as I shoot frame after frame.

When we're finished, Chris's mom says earnestly, "Why, you've certainly changed our ideas of what New Yorkers are like." We smile politely. We don't ask what those ideas might have been.

SCRATCH ANKLE

Alabama
Chris McKinley, tour guide

Kari, a young single mom, brings her two kids to the shoot. Her husband was killed two years ago in what she calls an "under ride"—an accident in which a car goes under the back end of a tractor-trailer.

Boring, it seems, is as advertised. "It really is boring here," Kari says. "What people do is sit on their steps and count cars." We find a set of old, red half-round steps next to an old blue building and have her sit on them. She asks, "Do you know what this building is?" She leans real close and whispers so her kids can't hear, "It's the local titty bar." She blushes slightly, and so do I. I reassure her that the building will not show, only the steps and the wild grass popping up into the frame. It's as lonesome a scene as I can cook up on short notice.

I start the shoot with a portrait lens, an 80-200mm telephoto zoom, but I switch to a 20mm wide-angle so I can include in the frame a bit of sky and the cars on the road, to give the picture more of Boring's atmosphere.

BORING
Oregon
Kari Hagan, mother of two

W e arrive half an hour early for our appointment to photograph Carol Lee Whiting in Flushing, which is maybe fifteen minutes away from my New York City studio. We eat up the time by driving around the neighborhood.

Carol tells us that when she was a little girl in this neighborhood it was populated mostly by Scottish, Polish, and African American families. Now it's mainly Asian. The only problem, according to Carol, is that the store signs feature only Asian characters, and the locals are trying to make it a requirement that some English appear on the signs so that everybody will know what kind of business is going on inside each store. There is a strong sense of community in Flushing, she says.

Carol is a retired English teacher who has been selected by the local community board to be their historian. The appointment just happened so she's not yet up to speed and can't tell us how Flushing got its name.

Throughout the session Carol is cheerful and cooperative, displaying a broad, engaging smile that just won't quit. I would have preferred her over three teachers I had when I was in school.

FLUSHING
New York
Carol Lee Whiting, retired teacher

We drive up the panhandle of Idaho through spectacular scenery. The U.S. portion of the highway terminates at the Canadian border, only two miles from the town of Good Grief, where we find the Good Grief Tavern closed and no one in sight. We drive 35 miles south to Bonner's Ferry and ask the sheriff if he can help us find a volunteer to photograph up at the tavern. He suggests one of his sergeants, George Voyles, who agrees to meet us up the highway at the 247-mile marker just as soon as he takes his cruiser to the car wash. He knows every milepost in the county because while there's almost no crime up here there are a lot of accidents. It seems that giant, off-balance logging trucks don't mix well with Canadian tourists speeding down the highway to Bonner's Ferry, where there's a Kootenai tribal casino.

Smug in our knowledge that the only patrol car in the area is getting washed, we race to the mile marker at well over the posted limit. We set up and when the good sergeant arrives he puts on his tough-cop sunglasses and points the radar gun down the highway. The sergeant tells us that the gun is used on this stretch of road to monitor the speed of Canadians driving down to the casino. He adds, "We only check them on their way to the casino. Most don't have any money on the return trip."

The picture looks awesome in the viewfinder, but I've had years of experience seeing *viewfinder awesome* turn to *light-table awful,* so I try not to think too much about the possibility of a great photo.

We wrap it up, the sergeant signs the model release form, and with him standing by the roadside with his radar gun, we stay well under the speed limit as we drive away.

GOOD GRIEF

Idaho
Sergeant George Voyles, police officer

At the Eureka Inn we ask the desk clerk if he knows anyone who might be willing to pose for a photo. He doesn't hesitate. With zeal and genuine conviction, he says that his grandfather, Bob Brown, is the man we're looking for. A man of character, with an animated, expressive face, the grandson says, and a local artist to boot. It seems his sculpted metal bugs were the talk of the town back in the early '80s. As a matter of fact, he's known as the Bug Man.

How can we go wrong with someone called the Bug Man? We make arrangements to meet Bob the next morning.

When he arrives at the inn he tells us he was an oyster farmer and a teacher of disabled children. He used his metal-working talent to weld a wheelchair to his bicycle so he could speed the kids around town and let them feel the wind in their faces.

He takes us to a shopping center where three of his sculptures stand in the morning mist. They were commissioned by the developer of the small mall. Bob says, "Two were to be abstract and symbolic of the Earth in its raw stage and in its developing stage. The third was to be a more literal piece, showing the developer's parents as settlers casting their seeds on the earth."

I choose to shoot him in front of the Earth-in-its-raw-stage sculpture, as it pretty much matches the mood of the weather.

The mist is so thick that it soaks us in minutes as we search for a decent angle, but Bob remains filled with good cheer and stories. He pours out tale after tale of local events in which he's participated, including a people-powered sculpture race that has become an international affair.

After the pictures we duck into the front seat of Bob's car to keep dry, and it's then that I discover the secret of his prodigious memory: he has prepared pages of handwritten notes! He must have been up all night, filling the pages of yellow legal pads with a lifetime of names, dates, and stories. We're in for a long chat here as Bob fills us in on everyone and everything about Eureka. About the only thing he doesn't know is the origin of the town's name. The most logical story would have a miner reaching into a stream, plucking up a shiny nugget, and yelling . . . well, you know.

Bob's last nugget of local history is inspired by the morning's weather. "Eureka is so foggy that, during World War II, the Air Corps trained their England-bound pilots to fly in fog by bringing 'em here."

EUREKA

California

Bob Brown, sculptor

We roll into Panic on a made-to-order, chamber-of-commerce-calendar day: warm with dry air and a sunny sky complete with puffy cumulous clouds. The hills and valleys are green with sweet corn and the pastures are filled with horses and cows.

We round a bend on the rising blacktop and pass a tiny sign proclaiming this unpopulated piece of farmland road to be "The Town of Panic." At the crest of the hill is a small tractorlike vehicle to which is hitched a cart filled with corn. The tractor has a patio umbrella strapped to it, which shades the reclining figure of a teenage boy reading a dirt bike magazine. We find out that he's Scott Baer, and his dad parked him at this corner to sell the family corn and thereby "learn the value of a buck."

This bucolic scene, with umbrella tassels dancing in the breeze, the postcard sky filled with clouds, and the rolling cornfields framing the supine teenager, is, of course, the visual antithesis of panic. But photographers rely on two basic questions: Got light? Got any kind of picture? If the answer to either is yes, the rule is: Shoot it now!

We pose Scott in a hard-to-hold position while we fiddle with lenses, tripods, reflectors, and, eventually, a small flash setup. We get a few rolls but I'm missing that elusive warm feeling that says, "Wow! That was it!"

We try different lighting and a different lens. Scott is getting worn out holding the pose. With everything finally set up we discover that the brand-new batteries we use to fire the remote flash units—fully tested two days before—are mysteriously dead. All of them.

Then the only large cloud in seventy miles of sky covers the sun. And a customer stops to buy corn and parks his car in the scene. Eventually the cloud passes, and the scene empties. I figure a way to use a flash on my camera, and we shoot a few rolls.

Later, a visit with a local bank officer, who is also the local historian, reveals the origin of the town's name. It seems that sometime in the 1870s the town's denizens were sitting around drinking at a local watering hole when one of them said it was time to name this place. Another man was chewing a plug of tobacco, and he waved the package around. In keeping with what was a common custom of naming commercial goods, this brand of tobacco had been named by the manufacturer after the hard times of the post–Civil War period. It was called Panic Plug. "Why not name it Panic?" the man offered, not realizing that his fellow citizens were so toasted they'd find his joking suggestion a fine idea.

It's a first for us, visiting a town named after a plug of chewing tobacco.

PANIC

Pennsylvania

Scott Baer, student, roadside vendor

Dull, Ohio, is a tiny community outside the hamlet of Ohio City. Ohio City's claim to fame is that it's the place where the gasoline-powered automobile was invented. It is also, we are told, the location of the first automobile accident. Dull turns out to be a stretch of farm road and a few houses. It is flat, and green with August crops.

It's starting to rain as we drive past a highway department road sign announcing that "Six Houses Make a Dull Town." We slow down to wave at two Dull residents, who wave back from their porch. They turn out to be Shirley and Billie Clark. Billie is a burly retired corrections officer whose job it was to escort escapees back to prison. He laughs easily and is quick to announce all sorts of facts about the town of Dull and about every aspect of his life since an injury got him sent home from the Korean War. He is expert at slipping bad jokes into the stream of his personal history. Shirley is central casting's Ohio Grandma: round, sweet, and plainly dressed, with an easy laugh and a twinkle in her eye.

Billie tells us that Dull was named in the 1890s after James Martin Dull, a general-store owner and popular merchant who was also a huckster. Hucksters drove big wagons around from farm to farm, picking up fresh chickens, eggs, and produce to barter with other farmers.

The community was then known as McKee, but since there was a bigger McKee elsewhere in the state, the government asked the town fathers to select a new name for the official post office. Apparently it was a no-brainer: Dull was chosen in honor of the town's leading citizen. And so went the fate of the lesser McKee.

I ask Billie if he and Shirley will pose for a picture on their porch swing, sitting on the American flag afghan that's already draped on the slatted wood. Billie laughs and says, "Gee, you want me to break your camera? Suppose I just sit there looking slack-jawed with my mouth open since this is Dull. Shirley, whattya think? Shall we do that?" Of course, he's figured out my secret agenda and is offering to do exactly what I had in mind.

Shirley's feet don't reach the deck and the look is terrific. They do some very blank-faced poses, then lose the mask and let their natural charm show through.

We say our good-byes at least seven times. Billie will not let us go without reliving his varied and interesting life. We listen until the stories reach re-runs, then we beg off and drive away.

DULL

Ohio

Billie Clark, retired corrections officer, and his wife, Shirley

Trying to find Ding Dong, we drive right past it. The folks at our motel, only twelve miles away, have never heard of it. I'm sweating at the thought that we've driven over two thousand miles to get here and maybe there is no "here."

Matt spots a row of empty-looking store fronts and a dance hall, the Ding Dong Palace. Apparently this is the Ding Dong business district. We find the church, which is a few mobile homes and a small house with a sign at the bottom of the driveway that proclaims the opportunity for "uninterrupted prayer." Two teens in a car will tell us only that this *is* Ding Dong, before speeding off. A white Cadillac stops and a well-to-do sort asks in a "what the hell are you doing here" tone what we're looking for. We begin to tell him, but he makes a face that indicates he wants nothing to do with whatever it is. Matt and I agree that this is a spooky, out of synch place that may be populated by folks in the witness protection programs.

We drive twelve miles to the next town, where I ask the quick-stop counter man if he knows anybody who lives in Ding Dong. "Nope," he says. I ask if he knows anybody who knows anybody who lives in Ding Dong. He says that his boss knows about Ding Dong. I ask when the boss will be back and the guy nudges his head in the general direction of the juice coolers, indicating that the man standing a few feet away is the boss. I expect a rebuff or indifference, but I hit pay dirt. The boss is a member of the Ding Dong Volunteer Fire Department, and he tells me that the chief would probably be happy to pose for us next to the town's fire trucks.

The next morning, when the sun is millimeters above the horizon line, the rich dawn light and the Caribbean-blue sky combine to make the old fire engines look stately. We ask Harold Rowe, carpet salesman and Ding Dong fire chief, to climb into his yellow bunker pants and boots. With his bright red suspenders against a blue T-shirt, we now have the primary colors covered.

We learn that Ding Dong got its name when the Bell brothers, owners of the general store, petitioned the local government to name the town Bell. Coincidentally, the store happened to be in Bell County, and the authorities thought that that was Bell enough and declined. So the Bell boys hung a sign on their store to taunt the officials: a big bell-shaped affair reading "Ding" on one side, "Dong" on the other.

With that information we leave Ding Dong behind . . . without ever shaking the feeling that something really weird was going on there.

DING DONG
Texas
Harold Rowe, carpet salesman, fire chief

We meet Sheriff John Henson of the Carter County Sheriff's Department inside a Texaco quick-stop market. Amid swirling clouds of Marlboro smoke, the seasoned patrol vet recalls the history of Bitter End. It seems there were some serious feuds on Buck Mountain that ultimately led to a showdown shoot-out between two families, an event referred to by locals as "the end of the feud." The bitter end, apparently.

As we're leaving, the sheriff tells us that in the old days things would get pretty rowdy up on the mountain, and a patrol car that was sent up there would most likely return with its lights shot right off the top.

Oh, boy. Gunfire. A real plus on any road trip.

Deep in the hills we meet Terry and Jack Harrison, two young gents sporting long mountain-man beards, who pop out of the darkness of a small barn. After a brief explanation, Jack seems interested in posing and Terry willing to go along with his brother. Their beards are refreshingly disturbing. I can't decide if they make the Harrisons look like biblical characters or something a lot less holy.

Our Tennessee volunteers cope with harsh reflector glare until tears are produced, which is my signal to stop shooting and thank them. They happily sign releases, and then they tell me that they think the name Bitter End comes from the local hickory nuts, which local girls eat, resulting in a bitter taste when boys kiss them. It sounds like more story than history, but you never know.

So as to how Bitter End got its name, take your pick: fightin' or kissin'.

BITTER END
Tennessee
Terry and Jack Harrison, potato farmers

From a Road Warrior's Diary

What's always difficult is hotel research—that is, finding clean, low-priced rooms with phone jacks so I can post my daily online road journal. We're on a tight budget, so I employ every guise I can, including the old standby, the charming cheapskate. Over the phone I dance with all the reservation clerks in order to find the cheap rooms (asking for inexpensive rooms will simply get me the normal rate). I ask for any unadvertised "specials" or employ my AAA or AARP membership discounts. If it's a hotel chain, I always call both the toll free reservation number *and* the local property to test the given rates against one another. I also ask for no-smoking rooms. Forget to do that and I risk the unmistakable combination of stale tobacco and aerosol potpourri with just a hint of male cat spray, the stench that upon opening the door to the room brings a tear to my eye and a roll to my stomach. Not to say that the room I'll get will actually be one in which no smoking has taken place, just that it'll be a room in which they've used the *expensive* room deodorant.

On the way to Pig, Kentucky, we see two memorable signs. One is a giant yellow billboard on the interstate that urges us to "Visit the Boobie Bungalow." We pass on the invitation but spend a lot of time wondering about what we might have seen there.

In Texas we're told that we'll save an hour by driving the back roads to El Paso. I'm skeptical. Back roads can get real slow, what with cautious school busses and amblin' farmers. But we try it and end up averaging eighty-five miles an hour on the straightest, smoothest two-lane blacktop I've ever seen. The occasional slow driver sees us coming and pulls over so we can pass. It seems to be a local courtesy. We're flyin' and there are no police. I guess these roads are so lightly traveled that there's no money to be gained in the enforcement of the speed limit.

❋

There are a lot of little packing tricks a true road warrior learns after years spent pursuing pictures. One of mine is the perfect shampoo bottle. Small, it will nevertheless hold a two-week supply of my own shampoo, and it will not leak all over my electric shaver or alarm clock because of its secure top that clicks open easily at the touch of a thumb. This marvel is the bottle that Johnson & Johnson uses for its No More Tears Baby Shampoo. A few days ago it slipped off the skimpy shelf in the motel shower and fell to the tub floor, denting the oval bottom. Now it won't stand up too well. This morning it tips over and falls onto the top of my foot causing much pain, so before we hit the road, we stop at a Wal-Mart and buy a replacement. Now there's no more tears from head to foot. My Professional Photography Road Kit is now once again complete.

❋

The Trooper is equipped with a CB radio, which allows us to evade the highway patrolmen (whom truckers call Smokies) or, at the very least, to adjust our speed when they're around. The trucks on the interstate hustle along at seventy to eighty-five miles an hour. We pass most of them. Thanks to the CB we are ticket free but inundated with trucker's lingo and wild discussions for many a long stretch of interstate. One thing we learn is to say a laconic "pie-shite it," which means we're thankful for something someone has done for us.

❋

In rural Alabama we enter a town where the official sign reads, "Magnolia, Alabama. Home of the Magnolia Post Office." We look at each other. Where else would we expect it to be?

❋

The trance that's induced by hours of driving while listening to bad local radio can free your mind to wander into semi-dream territory. While rolling along Interstate 80 in Pennsylvania between the towns of Fearnot and Panic, we notice the strangest series of lines painted across the highway's granny lane (for non-truckers, that's the slow lane). The lines are grouped in batches of twenty or so, and they alternate in color between yellow and white and vary in thickness from fairly wide to quite narrow. I've never seen anything like them before, and I wonder if they are some kind of speed control markings, intended to be seen by police aircraft passing above.

Then I have a travel-trance-induced revelation: This is God's bar code, and we are cruising down His checkout lane. I slow down. After three miles, the lines end. Confident that we aren't going to be plucked up and bagged, I resume our normal pace.

Road trance turns into stupor when I stop at a mini-mart/gas station to fuel the car and use the rest room. Matt lounges against a nearby railing to guard the gear and have a cigarette. I walk into the single-occupancy facility and lock the door. It is one of the cleanest gas station rest rooms I've ever seen. There's even a can of air freshener. There's no urinal, just a toilet. Must be the result of some new political correctness thing. I take care of business, wash up, dry my hands, and open the door to the blazing sun and a view of a man standing near Matt. The man's knees are pressed together and he's hopping slightly in place with that unmistakable "I've got to get in there right now!" expression on his face, an expression that changes to one of complete incredulity when he sees me. Matt looks at me and says, "What are you doing in the ladies'

I just told this guy that he couldn't get into the men's because it was occupied. I thought you were in there!" The guy is now cross-eyed with urgency. Matt turns to him and, sounding like a john cop directing toilet traffic, says, "OK, sir, you can go in now."

Before every trip we attend to the Trooper: check the tires, change the oil, remove accumulated trunk junk. Stash the little air compressor. Load up on tire sealant, coolers, bungee cords. Pack a modified tool kit for the long desert stretches. Get out the Club, hide the Mace. Get extra keys for Matt so when I lose mine we can still drive on.

The Trooper's windows sport the world's greatest (in my opinion) warning stickers. These laminated labels, made with the best typography, formatting, and art my computer can provide, read: **ORBITNAV™ SATELLITE TRACKING. WARNING! THIS VEHICLE'S MOVEMENTS ARE CONTINUOUSLY TRACKED AND RECORDED BY ORBITNAV™ [LOGO] REALTIME HUNTER GPS SATELLITE SYSTEMS. LOCATOR KEY 0782230987A #2247-22 <BAR CODE> CZ925 3/00 NT.**

They look so official that people regularly ask me where they can get information about my security system.

You may not know this, but New Yorkers have to make special preparations to enter the heartland of America. You don't just rush willy-nilly through the Lincoln Tunnel and expect to survive. You begin by purging your thoughts and conversations of hicks-from-the-sticks jokes and observations. Only when this is accomplished can meaningful, respectful interaction with those who reside outside Manhattan take place. This purging usually happens during the first hour or two on the road and involves various unkind references to farming, slow speaking, and tractor caps.

It doesn't help that on one trip, just two hours southwest of New York, we pull up behind a convoy of modular homes on wheels. "You know you're in the boonies when you see someone's house on the road," Matt says. "And I mean literally on the road."

We have a good day in Hell.

When we arrive we meet Jim Ley, the self-proclaimed mayor, who tells us, "I won by one vote. Mine." Jim's a sharp promoter who's been successfully marketing the name of the town for years. Hell lore tells of a local landowner from a few generations ago named Reeves, a raucous fellow known to party hard and frequently, who tried to give the town his own name. The other residents objected and blocked his efforts. He got real mad, and at a town meeting shouted, "You all can go to hell, and you can call this place Hell for all I care." You can guess the rest.

Mayor Jim and his wife, Rose, own the general store in Hell. It's called the Devil's Den, and it's painted fire-engine red. As the president of the local chamber of commerce, he presides over a variety of functions and holds the postmaster position. He also operates an official weather station for the U.S. Weather Bureau. I wonder if his reports ever include statements like "Today the entire region will be hot as Hell."

Jim has a trunk full of hell jokes and an endless supply of stories about interviews he's had with journalists from all over the world. He tells about a man who came to his store one autumn and asked if he could use the little park behind the Devil's Den for an outdoor wedding the following January. Jim said, "Sure, but why in the middle of winter?" The guy replied, "Well, I told all my friends it would be a cold day in hell when I got married."

We pose Jim and Rose sitting on the logs that surround the store's roadside billboard. I abandon my humanity and go for the editorial jugular by throwing reflected light up from the ground. It works and they look devilish but happy. I think—and sort of hope—that their warmth will override my lighting.

We stop for gas and Cokes before leaving. When I look at the change handed to me by the quick-stop market attendant, I see that one of the dollar bills has a child's handwriting on it: "For God, from Ann R."

I take Ann's dollar out of Hell.

HELL
Michigan
Mayor Jim Ley and his wife, Rose

After six hours of driving in perfect photography weather we reach our destination just as the postcard-pretty sky turns a murky green with clouds spewing hail, heavy rain, and multiple spikes of lightning.

Welcome to Suckerville, pilgrim.

Previously I'd talked to the editor of a local newspaper, and he'd arranged for me to photograph Miriam Bisbee, a seventy-five-year-old columnist for the paper and a chronicler of local history. The editor thinks I'll be hard-pressed to find a good site at which to shoot because, he says, all there is in Suckerville is a big rock upon which all the young locals have painted their names.

We beat the rain by waiting it out, deciding to shoot the next morning. But we can't beat the rock for a photo location. Unfortunately it sits at the side of a curving two-lane back country road with high-speed local traffic coming in both directions. My mind pictures the disaster that befell Stephen King a few years ago: struck by a van while walking on a road exactly like this, he was almost killed. Years of covering accidents for local newspapers makes me fearful; photo shoots are rubbernecking magnets that can easily create highway disasters.

Along with Miriam several local volunteers have come to help us, and I press them into service to shout a warning every time a car approaches. We settle into a routine of shooting a few frames from the center of the road, then hearing shouts and running for cover.

Miriam reports that the town got its name from nearby Sucker Creek, which is populated by fish called suckers.

When I ask her if the people of the town get upset about all the garish painting on this rock, which is set in such a scenic place, she replies, "This is a very polite town and we don't usually go along with this sort of thing, but this curve is an accident waiting to happen. You want to be stone-cold sober when you drive around the curve on this road. The rock gets your attention."

SUCKERVILLE

Maine

Miriam Bisbee, newspaper columnist, local historian

Fleatown is a strange mix of humble homes near the highway and wealthy estates and farms set back a respectable distance from the road. We boldly drive up to a big farmhouse and meet the owner, David Schell, who is standing outside grinning at us. He's either very friendly or nuts. Turns out he's the former, and before I get half a question about Fleatown out of my mouth, he starts talking. He's got a great sense of humor and understands exactly what we're doing. His wife, Jane, is smiling as he introduces her.

They're not too clear on how Fleatown got its name, but they think that it may have come from the fact that at one time the town was the location of an overnight stagecoach stop and an animal farm. He reports that rather than being embarrassed by the name locals are secure enough to flaunt it for fun.

I want to pose them in front of the wall of the green barn and include a small white window in the frame. I ask David to change his light tan shirt for a red one because I can't resist shooting red and green together. We lure Gracie, the Schells' golden lab, into the picture with hot dogs.

Just as I'm about to take the picture Gracie starts to scratch herself. I don't believe my eyes as the photo I wished for happens. I shoot two of the fastest rolls of film I've ever shot in my life. I swear I smell smoke coming from the back of the camera.

David and Jane are laughing. I hear Matt laughing from behind the reflector we're using to throw more light on Gracie. Even a nearby farm hand is laughing.

We say our good-byes with many thank-yous and a promise to send prints.

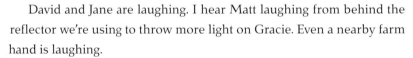

FLEATOWN
Ohio
David and Jane Schell, farm owners, and Gracie

Rescue turns out to be a town totally without quaintness, a featureless little stretch of road between two other towns.

We discover a schoolteacher who is painting the small rooms in the tiny schoolhouse. When we ask about the town's name, she shrugs, but when we ask her about a person to pose for us we have better luck. She tells us to visit Frank, her father-in-law, who lives down the street. He's eightyish, rugged, and dressed in overalls, his face weathered from working on the town road crew. Today is so hot he's stayed off the job. He doesn't have any idea how the town got its name but thinks our project sounds "just fine," and he agrees to pose the next day in front of an abandoned one-room schoolhouse on a nearby road. We ask him to bring a shovel or some other road-work tool with him so we can use it as a prop. I'm thinking that having him lean on something would help him look and feel relaxed.

In the morning we're running late for our appointment with Frank and I'm afraid he'll decide not to wait for us and take off for work. As we speed to the abandoned school, we fall in behind a giant road grader that's lumbering up the road at about four miles an hour. I nervously check my watch. We finally reach a spot where I can safely pass the behemoth machine, and as I zoom by, dust flying, I look over and see Frank high up in the cab. Matt and I realize that to a road crew worker, a grader is known as a shovel. Frank did exactly what I asked—he brought his shovel to the shoot.

RESCUE
Missouri
Frank Reynolds, road worker

On our way into town we pass a sign claiming to mark the birthplace of George Washington's mother.

Herb and Marnie meet us at their real estate office on the edge of the Potomac River near Stinking Point at 8:00 A.M. Herb, a lifelong native, tells us that Stinking Point was named as a result of the sinking of a Union prison ship during the Civil War. The dead washed ashore and got pretty pungent because nobody cared enough to bury the bodies. Finally, a group of slaves volunteered to do the job if they could keep the gold buttons they found on officers' tunics.

Herb and I stroll across the fog-shrouded lawn of a house for sale on the river. We walk to a tiny point jutting out into the water. It's easy to imagine bodies getting caught in the tangled tree roots that curl around the beach.

Even though the area's houses are empty, I feel like I'm trespassing. Then I notice that Herb and Marnie are both sporting clipboards and, because people with clipboards are always official, I begin to feel official too.

A thin ray of sunlight splashes down through a hole in the clouds. In that perfect pool of sun, Herb and Marnie, looking every bit the ideal real estate team, smile and hold their clipboards. The grass glows electric green in the low-angled, early-morning light. The Potomac, shrouded in deep mist only moments earlier, glitters gold from the sun's glare.

On the way out of town, we pass a roadside restaurant with a sign that reads "Bullets: Chicken and More."

"Bullets and pullets," Matt says. "Yummy."

STINKING POINT

Virginia

Herb and Marnie Barnes, business owners

I t's raining hard and the prospects for a good shoot in Nuttsville are dim. We get alternating weather patterns on our seven-hour trip to the town. One moment it's dark and raining and I'm figuring possible shots in my head using my new battery-powered flash system. Then the sun pops out and I immediately segue into shots that can be done with the reflector. I go back and forth like this maybe twenty times during the trip.

But we luck out in Nuttsville, finding Tracey Cooper, a tall, attractive young woman who says she's the local splash artist. I ask her what that is and she responds, "I paint houses." I shoot her for about an hour. The new lights work flawlessly.

We talk to several people but nobody is willing to say for sure how Nuttsville got the name, although most agree that the earliest owner of the general store was named William D. Nutt.

The locals don't have a town sign. People keep stealing it.

NUTTSVILLE

Virginia

Tracey Cooper, splash artist

The winding narrow roads around Odd are heavily traveled by semis and coal trucks that ooze over the white line as they rumble down the skinny two-lane highway. From years of shooting in the mines for energy clients I remember how scary these roads are. Driving on them keeps my pulse rate up.

Odd consists of a few houses and a post office, which is closed because it's Sunday. Houses around here sit right out next to the road because the roads in this part of coal country follow the skinny valleys cut by streams between the hills creating the only level land. The hills are so steep that building more than a few feet away from the road is all but impossible.

No one we talk to wants to pose, and neither does anyone have a clue about the origin of the town's name. In fact, they don't think the name is odd at all and they can't understand our interest.

We notice an old gent on his front porch. He's sitting between two plastic swan planters and a worn-out washing machine. We stop, talk, and discover that he's John Monk, a retired coal miner. He says, "Twenty-five years in the mine and I guess I got lucky and escaped the black lung."

He knows nothing about the town's name, but he loves posing and laughs almost the whole time. We use a silver and gold reflector to aim a little light under the eaves of his porch. As soon as I stop to reload film, he stops being animated and goes into torpor mode. The minute I fire off the first frames and the camera starts making its motor-drive noises, he snaps into full smiling-and-talking mode. We tell him that he is just like the professional models we work with. He thinks that's hogwash, but it's not.

ODD

West Virginia

John Monk, retired coal miner

We drive aimlessly, looking for any sign of life in this rural area. When I spot a car pulling into a driveway, I zoom in behind and begin my spiel. The man smiles as I start talking, and I know we have a live one. He tells us his name is Curtis Ward and he's a bail bondsman. We make arrangements to photograph him the following morning.

The sun is edging its way over the trees on the horizon as we pull into Curtis's driveway. It's the golden hour of the morning, but Curtis's wife says he's off on a mission of some sort and will be right back. We watch the long shadows get shorter, bleeding the rosy color out of the scene a little at a time.

Finally, Curtis pulls in and we push him into high gear. He puts on a wonderful-looking green getup replete with stripes, badges, and a menacing sidearm. He's suddenly Mr. Law Enforcement, the look more bounty hunter than bail bondsman. I smile at the tiny golden handcuffs that serve as his tie pin.

We plunk him down in an old, shabby rocker on his lawn, and I shoot him close up. He is a sweet-looking man, and the paramilitary outfit contrasts with his smile, which manages to break through the serious faces I coax out of him. Even when he's holding his big silver gun, there's a hint of fun in his face.

After about six rolls Curtis takes us up the road to visit Miss Theo Sherrill, the local authority on Shorts. She tells us that the name came from the Shorts Baptist Church, which got its name from the Shorts family back in the early 1800s. She remembers her father telling her that a visiting preacher once returned home and got into trouble with his wife when he told her that he had spent the day "preachin' in Shorts."

SHORTS
Alabama
Curtis Ward, bail bondsman

We're told that Steve Waller, a mill worker, part-time preacher, and horse breeder, has built a full-sized wooden model of a horse that he uses for a mailbox. On our way to take his photo, we spend much of the time speculating about where the postman puts the mail. When we meet up with him he poses next to his mailbox, which turns out to be a flat, painted board fashioned to resemble a horse—and it's the creature's head that opens to receive mail.

Our expectations defeated, we ask around about the origin of the town's name and are told that early settlers, the Edwin Hickman family, lived on a creek in what is now Hickman County. The local Native Americans apparently wanted these folks gone, and they launched an attack that some say lasted four days, resulting in the deaths of all the family members. The creek was subsequently named Defeated Creek, and later the town took the name too.

Edwin Hickman was buried on the creek, and his grave site became a historic feature of the area. It did not, however, become sacred ground, because in later years the town dug him up and moved him to another resting place in order to accommodate a new bridge.

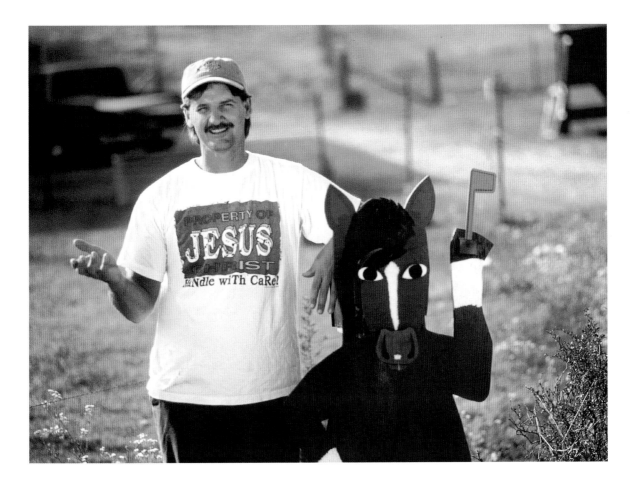

DEFEATED
Tennessee
Steve Waller, preacher, mill worker, horse farmer

To go to War we dive deep into coal country on the narrowest roads I've ever seen in the United States. The turns are so sharp that we slow to maybe eight or ten miles an hour in order to handle the tight switchbacks. There's a lot of jabbing at the brake pedal, and Matt's getting carsick from the relentless side-to-side motion. The oncoming coal trucks menace anyone driving near the mid-stripe. It's mind-numbingly slow progress mixed with heart-jolting fright whenever these behemoths hurtle by within inches of our fender.

In War we find a once-thriving city that shrank from a population of three thousand to less than a third of that when the big coal companies closed down in the '80s. War got its name from a four-day-long battle between a group of Shawnees and a settler back in the 1800s that locals termed "more like a war than a fight."

We've called ahead and are met by a van loaded with VFW officials. For our portrait subject we choose Gillio Ferrante, who was a turret gunner in a B-17 bomber in World War II. He stands proudly in the street, War's police department in the background. When I ask Gillio to salute for the photo, he snaps a great one that's easily fifty years younger than his seventy-eight years.

WAR
West Virginia
Gillio Ferrante, retired brick mason, veteran

Fresno is a sleeping and eating spot on our way to Tranquillity, which, true to its name, is peaceful and pleasant, but not brimming with picture possibilities. I know this can work in either of two ways: a serene, thoughtful portrait that reflects the name, or a photo that's loud and noisy and plays off the contrast. But as I stumble around during our scouting session, I see nothing that's fun, exciting, or strange.

I notice a gardener using a gas-powered weed whacker. Now we're cookin'—if he's got ear protectors on, we'll have our contrast photo. But he's not wearing them, and I walk away thinking he'll be deaf by forty.

I see nothing. I feel like a comedian who has just walked on stage to a round of applause and had his mind go completely blank. I don't have a single thought about how to make a picture here.

Folks at the local school are totally disinterested in what we're doing and have no idea about the origin of the town's name.

Eventually I walk into a Buick dealership to use the rest room and get a Coke from the machine. A demure, gray-haired woman dressed in tweed asks if she can help me. She's Virginia Burns, owner of the dealership, and she seems friendly (but what Buick dealer doesn't?).

She agrees to pose for us and I make the pictures with her standing across the street with the most tranquil of puffy-cloud-filled skies as a backdrop.

As a bonus, she has a story to tell about the town's name. It seems that two farmers were fighting over where to locate a new farm-supply and general store because having the store a mile or two closer to one farm or the other would offer a big advantage. (The store owner would be building on one of the farmers' property.) They battled so long that the townspeople wondered if they'd ever get the store they needed. Finally they agreed to place the store squarely on the borderline between the two farms. The store was named the Tranquillity Store because finally there was no more warring between the two farmers.

TRANQUILLITY
California
Virginia Burns, car dealer

n Tight Squeeze we meet with Glen Giles and his wife, Pat. Glen is a historian who tells us that Tight Squeeze got its name in the nineteenth century when a narrow dirt road linking Washington, D.C., and Atlanta ran through the area. All day long teams of horses pulled wagonloads of goods to be sold in one city or the other. At one point on the road a blacksmith shop and a general store faced each other across the trail. The general-store owner built a massive portal that extended out from the store over part of the roadway so that carriages could stop and women passengers could walk inside on rainy days without getting their shoes muddy. Not to be outdone, the blacksmith built his version of a courtesy awning; it, too, extended well over the roadway. What was left of the passage was so narrow that teams of horses could only just squeeze through, and so the town's name came into being. Despite lots of off-color jokes about the name, the town's merchants have always prevailed against attempts to change the name. The moniker Tight Squeeze, it seems, is good for business.

Glen and Pat are celebrating their forty-sixth anniversary, but they are still as cuddly as a couple of teenagers. I ask them to pose in a rusted glider chair in front of a faded red barn. On an ideal morning the low rising sun would wash across the scene, but this day has dawned overcast, drizzly, and drab. I stick with the location, though, and Glen and Pat snuggle in and laugh and smile their way through the shoot. I thought couples like this existed only in the minds of sitcom writers, but here they are, real happy, nice, loving folks.

After the shoot Glen and Pat invite us to join them at the Tight Squeeze Hardee's, where they usually meet with friends to eat breakfast and chat. We spend two hours with the group, then we take off for the next town on our list.

TIGHT SQUEEZE
Virginia
Glen Giles, historian, and his wife, Pat

The trip to Zero requires thirteen hours of driving the interstate and an overnight in Bozeman. When we cross from Idaho to Montana, the scenery changes. It's big sky country and the view is a hundred miles in all directions with mountain ranges in every quadrant. The sky is thrilling. Out here the ranches that border the interstate are the size of counties. To get on or off the highway, we must cross cattle grates. This is one place where they don't want the buffalo to roam.

Montana has no speed limit, so we edge up to ninety on the smooth, straight road. We get to Zero and find it's an abandoned gas station and garage. Nearby are early '50's Chevys, Buicks, and Pontiacs, chrome chariots languishing in high spring grass.

We stop at the local bar. No one has any idea of how the town got to be called Zero, but we're told that Bob Lausch, who once owned the Zero Garage, which we'd passed earlier, spends his time weaving endless stories for anyone who'll listen. We meet up with Bob, a seventy-six-year-old gent who talks with a slight slur, perhaps from a stroke, and walks with a cane because of a plastic hip on one side and a bad knee on the other. We say hello and that's about the last word we get in. Bob tells his stories virtually nonstop. But suddenly there's a split-second pause and we make our request. Bob agrees to pose for us and says he'll meet us at the old garage, which is twenty miles away, just as soon as he finishes a fresh beer.

Matt and I head for the car to get ahead of him so we can scout the area. I say that Bob is up to the trip and will be there in a half hour. Matt says one hour, if at all. We're both wrong. We speed at eighty-five miles an hour down the interstate and associated back roads for fifteen minutes. Bob arrives exactly one minute after we get there.

After thirty minutes of shooting I find myself lying in tall grass doing a low-angle shot. I think to ask the old-timer if there are any rattlesnakes around here. He says, "Not since they put the train tracks across the road. The coal trains vibrate the ground and the snakes hate that."

I keep on shooting and pray for train.

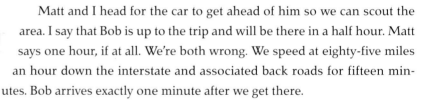

ZERO
Montana
Bob Lausch, retired garage owner

We've learned ahead of our visit that Suck-Egg Hollow got its name when a local egg farmer, angry that his eggs were being eaten by what he assumed were his neighbors' animals, began a shooting rampage. He shot neighbors' dogs and every other animal that moved anywhere near his henhouses. The toll mounted. So did the wrath of the neighbors. But before the neighbors took any retribution, the trigger-happy farmer discovered to his horror that the eggs were being eaten by black snakes and copperhead snakes. He apologized for the executions, admitting that it was the snakes that were "sucking down the eggs."

The morning's wet, dense fog lifts as we drive into Suck-Egg Hollow and make our way to the home of Garry DeVries, a chicken rancher and egg farmer. His wife, Tracy, is an ex-Yankee from Rochester, New York. They agree to let us shoot them and their young son, Jason, in a front-porch family portrait with their "Eggs For Sale" sign in full view. I want to put a fistful of fresh eggs in Garry's hands, but he thinks that the laying is over for the day and he won't have enough to hold. I tell him that we'll go to the general store and buy some. Everyone is silent. It's not a popular idea. We go with the few eggs we can muster.

SUCK-EGG HOLLOW

Tennessee

Tracy, Garry, and Jason DeVries, chicken and egg farmers

We meet azalea farmer Steve Tapp and spend an hour shooting in his greenhouse. Our subject is Lee Ann Rhea, a neighboring farmer who grows cotton and soy beans. She's a real farmer even though she looks, to this city slicker, like someone's suburban sister.

From the information we get, we learn that the town got its name from a popular local brand of cookies. In the early 1800s, a wealthy resident named John Henry Garnett, called Squire Garnett by the locals, opened a general store to serve the people who farmed in the region. In a status move, he asked a senator friend to petition the government on his behalf to get a local post office, and when he got it, for some reason unknown to everyone we met, he named the post office and the town after the cookies.

They must have been some cookies.

YUM YUM

Tennessee

Lee Ann Rhea, soy and cotton farmer

We get lucky and find three of the town's six residents sitting in tight formation in metal-tube lawn chairs under a shade tree next to a table of garage-sale items. They are so talkative and friendly that we can hardly get our request in edgewise.

When I ask why the sale is being held in the middle of the week, Jammie says, "Makes no difference—Tuesday, Saturday, we're here all the time, 'less it gets too hot. Then we slide into the shade."

Jammie tells us that the town got its name from a long-gone general store that served greasy burgers back in the '20s.

While we're talking, I notice that all three women flick glances at the table closest to the road where a city-dressed woman and her little daughter are scrutinizing a large crocheted doll. The women's sentences randomly trail off as they turn to see if their customer needs assistance. Their attention seems to have more to do with security than with attentive salesmanship, but that may just be the way I'm seeing it.

Also, I can't tell if these women are actually friendly or if it's just a permanent Sunbelt squint that makes them seem that way. They say things that sound like serious comments, but those squinty smiles make me wonder if I'm missing some humor an outsider wouldn't catch.

GREASY CORNER

Arkansas

Linda McCollum, Jammie Smith, and Ada Fisker, neighbors

Jello du Jour

While it's true we got to eat out every night, there were perils. Road food features textures like those of Nerf toys, seasoning to the lowest common denominator, heating to just above spring thaw, and timing that defies serendipity.

Some memories instantly come to mind:

North Carolina provided barbecued chicken breast with the flavor of bottled water; it was garnished with a topping of store-bought ketchup. The side dishes were cold mashed potatoes and gray lima beans.

In Tennessee I had the worst road dinner I've ever eaten. Matt elected to have a pizza delivered to his room, so I was on my own. It was too late to make it to a decent restaurant, so I relied on the make-my-own-dinner strategy that's worked well in the past. I'd go to the local supermarket and shop for ingredients, usually buying turkey breast, lettuce, mustard, fresh-baked rolls, and some plastic knives and forks.

Not fancy, but good enough to munch on while watching CNN on the motel television. This time, though, the plan failed. At the supermarket the bakery section featured a bread-looking product that turned out to have the taste as well as the consistency of upholstery stuffing, and the usually reliable brown mustard in a squeeze bottle produced a strange-tasting dark slurry that could have been called vinegar squirt.

At Bonnie's cafe in Gas, Kansas, we ordered dinner from a menu that reminded me of a diner's bill of fare in the movie *My Cousin Vinnie*, which consisted of three choices: Breakfast, Lunch, and Dinner. The Kansas menu, though, did have enough items to be called a menu. I noticed a listing for chicken breasts. I asked, "How do you do these?" The waitress said, "Oh, we just pull them right out of the freezer and chuck them on the grill." I decided to forgo that delicacy. I ordered the chopped steak, medium rare. The waitress said, "Oh, we can only give that to you medium well or well." So I changed my mind and went back to the chicken, which turned out to be really good. Freezer-to-grill, eh? Well, I thought, that might be something to think about for my next barbecue back home.

If there's anything worse than dinner in a small-town, Texas-roadhouse-theme restaurant, it's having to wait for a table in a small-town, Texas-roadhouse-theme restaurant. This one was in an Ohio town whose name I've forgotten. While we waited we dutifully ate our peanuts, tossed the shells at little buckets, and missed, which added to the decor of the ambiance-stricken eatery. Halfway through the toughest beef brochette I had ever encountered, I considered tossing the little skewered Kevlar jawbreakers into the buckets. This meal was supposed to be a treat after a tough day that began with a Continental breakfast at a Pennsylvania Best Western. (The fact that neither of us could figure out what continent the breakfast came from should have been a signal that things were heading downhill.)

On a logging highway in northern Idaho we passed a Mexican restaurant advertising burritos and fajitas. It came to me that only a few days ago we were a mile from the Mexican border, but I never noticed a restaurant there offering Idaho potato salad, as this one did.

In Demopolis, Alabama, I had breakfast at the only local restaurant open at 5:00 A.M. I ordered an onion and pepper omelette, orange juice, and coffee. I was one of two customers, so it was a mystery why it took thirty minutes for the order to arrive. When it did I saw what looked like a burnt chamois swimming in grease. I tried to blot it with a paper napkin, but it continued to ooze a thick, Parkay-like oil from its innards. I draped a paper napkin over it, ate the pale toast, tasted the warm, brown water in the coffee mug, paid the check, and bolted.

Looking back, I realize we spent an inordinate amount of time on the road thinking about food and talking about food. It was hard not to. We approached almost every meal with a mixture of anticipation and dread. Sitting down to each road meal was, like a second marriage, the triumph of hope over experience.

We travel through the incredible Sonoma Valley and Klamath Forest regions of California and Oregon, through scenery so beautiful it hurts to look at it. A voice in my head says, "Buy a panoramic camera!" We stop for a few shots, then push on to continue our ten-hour journey to Zig Zag, Oregon.

We scout Zig Zag and in the rain shoot a picture of Sherry Shamness, a waitress at the Zig Zag Tavern. She says, "I can add this to my resume. Barrel racer, band singer, licensed nurse, two marriages, two kids, now a model . . . or whatever this is I'm doing." Her boss, the tavern's owner, treats Matt and me to pizza, possibly because she's just nice or because we entertained the hell out of her dinner crowd by photographing Sherry in full view of everyone.

One customer, looking at our giant 54-inch silver reflector, says, "I thought you were making a commercial about a giant pizza with that thing!"

The town's name? Comes from the nearby Zig Zag River, which zigs and zags its way through the territory.

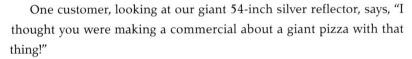

ZIG ZAG

Oregon

Sherry Shamness, waitress

We expect that a 7:00 A.M. Sunday breakfast at Ramona's Porky Pig Diner is going to be a pretty quiet affair, but when we walk in we see twenty men sitting around a large table having breakfast. Every head turns to look. I can almost hear their inner voices raising the alarm: "Strangers at seven o'clock!" There are no women here, so my guess is that the women do the Sunday church goin'.

On the walls are clusters of T-shirts and tractor hats, all bearing the name of the diner. They make the diner look like a thrift shop with food. A saw blade hand-painted with a local landscape hangs over the door to the john.

Ramona serves up scrambled eggs and a short stack and we dig in. She tells us that she has called the retired eighty-four-year-old owner of the original, now-closed, pig store, and her daughter-in-law.

When Rometta and Joan arrive they come right to our table without hesitation. Joan bellows at us, "Well, you look strange enough to be our visitors." They could be two characters right out of the old TV series *Golden Girls*. Rometta, who walks with a cane, is a dead ringer for Estelle Getty's character, Ma, right down to the giant glasses. Within moments, we're all acting like we've known each other for years.

Joan tells us how Pig got its name. It seems that sometime in the 1800s a resident's sow got wedged under the porch of the general store. Townspeople tried all day to rescue the squealing pig but succeeded only in getting dirty, smelly, and exhausted. It was finally decided that the best thing to do was to just let the pig stay stuck until it lost enough weight to be extracted, which is exactly what happened. Thereafter the general store was referred to as the pig store. Since the store was also the post office, when the government began bestowing official town names based on where the post office was located, the name Pig was awarded to the community.

After the story we chuckle our way through portrait sittings with Joan and Rometta.

PIG

Kentucky

Rometta Dawes and her daughter-in-law, Joan Wood

We can't resist stopping when we see on the map a town called Only, which turns out to be a falling-down general store with the owner, Alice E. Dyer, sitting inside in near darkness. Chair-ridden because of weight and arthritis, she oversees the only remaining enterprise in the one-room building, the remnant of the post office that was part of the general store, which prospered until Wal-Mart started selling goods cheaper than she could even buy them.

We photograph Alice in her chair by the light of the room's four 40-watt fluorescent bulbs. Matt stands in front of the window to block what little daylight seeps into the scene, to prevent it from affecting the balance of light.

Alice mentions that she thinks the town's name might have come from the fact that there were once two roads to the local school, and after one got paved, it became known as the only way to go, or the only road to the school—which would make sense because this general store was on that road too.

I know that the picture I've taken of Alice makes her look sad, but that's what I intended because that's the way the scene looked when I entered the room. But as I talk with Alice, her charming, folksy humor comes through, and I ask her if she'll move her chair and her little dog out onto the store's porch for a more cheerful, outdoor picture. She's happy to do that, and we take happier photographs.

Alice and her surroundings make me think about what it is I'm doing. As I'm shooting I wonder whether I'll choose a photo from inside or out. I decide I'll go with the most emotionally powerful image. I realize that this project is not about making flattering pictures. It's about showing what's there to be shown.

ONLY

Tennessee

Alice E. Dyer, postmaster

We find that at the exact corner our map gives us as the location of the town of Stuck is a scrapyard along the railroad tracks. We meet John David Sanderson, who runs the yard, and he says, "Yeah, sure, I know Stuck. It's just down the street over by the Stuck River." For years, he says, teens have organized beer parties there, and at every party someone gets a car stuck in the loose gravel and has to be towed out. Usually the cops show up and everyone gets busted. John David laughs at this story. "I was always with the guy who came to the party with a four-wheel drive. He would hook his winch up to a tree before the party and wait for some poor kid to get stuck, and then he would smile, hold up five fingers and shout, 'Five bucks and I'll tow you out before the cops come!'"

John David is having a wonderful time telling us the town's history. I ask him if he'll pose and he practically throws himself up on his forklift, which he lovingly calls "Mr. Aluminum Masher." He's terrific looking—a grimy, friendly guy grinning with the best teeth money can buy. He has a wonderful sparkle in his eyes. He's a natural, and we are instantly comfortable. After the shoot, we drive by the Stuck River thinking maybe we can take another picture of John David in the morning, but cancel this idea at the thought of seeing his big smile behind five fingers to get the Trooper out of the gravel.

STUCK

Washington

John David Sanderson, scrapyard owner

We arrive in Toast at about 7:00 P.M. It's been a seven-hour-plus haul and by the time we get there we *are* toast, but we still locate the two-chair barbershop where we're supposed to shoot tomorrow. It's closed. The barber who owns the shop is to be our subject, but we can't locate her to arrange a time.

The following morning we stand around the barbershop at 8:30 and watch good light get ugly. Our Toast talent is a no-show.

We've been on the road so long now that I have no idea what day it is. When I told a friend about my losing track of the days, he advised, "Check church parking lots. If they've got cars in 'em, it's Sunday." That's how we know today is Sunday—that and the fact that as we stand on the corner, every man, woman, and child passing by is dressed up. I think about going with them and asking God to send us a portrait subject.

Four volunteer firemen are drying hoses next door to the barbershop. I ask them if they'd like to pose. "Hay-ull no," says one, "but ol' Jeery over there will pose for you. He's honorary mayor of Toast." We find out later that the honorary mayor's name is Gary, but in these parts that's pronounced *Jeery*.

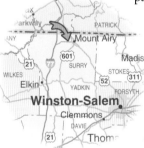

Gary comes over, smiles, and says he'll be happy to pose for a picture. He tells us he's the fire company's engineer and an iron worker and the chaplain of the fire company. He says, "I'm the chaplain for life. They can't take that away from me." There's a note of melancholy in his voice, and at that moment it occurs to me that he might not be fully competent. I realize that the good ol' boys have pulled a fast one on the out-of-towners. I feel a little sad that they used him to make a joke, but he is affable and looks interesting and so we photograph him.

Gary tells us that he really is the fire company engineer, but that he is not allowed to enter buildings at fires because, as he says, "they need me to keep the equipment running." From him we learn that Toast's claim to fame is Mount Airy, a mile away. Mount Airy is the hometown of Andy Griffith and the model for Mayberry, the town in the '60s-era TV show.

As far as the origin of the town's name goes, our research turns up two stories. One has it that Toast was an arbitrary name suggested in 1927 to postal authorities by the principal of the town's school. Another says that it had something to do with a fire in 1932 that left the center of town looking like burned toast.

TOAST

North Carolina

Gary Fore, fire department chaplain

As we cross from Pennsylvania into Ohio, Matt spots a town on the map called Delightful. We decide to check it out and find a church, a few houses, a cemetery, and an Ohio State Highway Patrol post. I see the photo right away: a tough trooper scowling into the camera with the Delightful Cemetery sign visible over his shoulder.

At the barracks, we win the confidence of Sergeant Joe Dragovich, who is squared-jawed, muscular, and very tough-looking indeed. His speech pattern goes this way: three sentences of friendly conversation, during which he can't disguise his interest in our project, then a quick snap back to cop-speak: "It sounds like a good idea, yes," he says. "I will do it. Please stand away from the desk and wait over there for me."

We shoot him looking fearsome in the frame. Over the sergeant's right shoulder is the sign from the cemetery across the narrow road. I grin my way through the shoot.

When I ask Sergeant Joe to sign a model release form, he says he has to show it to his superiors first. While he's doing this, we talk with the minister from the Delightful Church about how the town got its name. He explains that the town was once called Pleasant Hill, and it was run by a group of churchgoers who decided to honor a fellow preacher, one who just happened to become president of the United States: James A. Garfield. It seems Garfield was a minister who once came to the church of Pleasant Hill and, after preaching on a very hot day, sat and drank from the church's well. Finding the cool, clear water refreshing, he said, "This is delightful." Shortly after that Garfield became president. In his honor, the thrilled congregation voted to change the name of the tiny community to Delightful.

When Sergeant Joe returns he tells us that the Department of Safety will not allow him to sign the release. He says I'll have to petition the state for permission. And, if I don't mind, would I please hand over the film?

I'm stunned. But I smile and say, "I'll be happy to call them and get permission, but I'm sorry I can't give you the rolls of film because I have some images from yesterday's shoot on them." He smiles, letting on that he knows he can't legally seize the film. Then he asks if he can run my driver's license as a record of my visit. Nicely put, I think. A very professional, personable way to see if I'm on the run.

It turns out that the state of Ohio does license the use of the Highway Patrol's logo and the use of the faces of state employees. They're quite willing to issue a release for the purposes of my book. They say they'll send the paperwork to me in New York; all I have to do is fill it out and return it and in a month or so I'll receive the releases. How delightful.

DELIGHTFUL
Ohio
Sergeant Joe Dragovich, highway patrolman

Close your eyes and envision the smallest town you ever saw. Take away the commercial and farm buildings and leave just one tiny, thirty-foot-square structure. Now you've got Knockemstiff.

The one building is concrete-block affair with a hand-lettered sign that faces up the road: "Shake & Bake Tan and Women's Fitness." In the window of the locked front door is another handmade sign: "No Outside Lotions Permitted. Violators Will Pay."

It's early, and the low sun, rich with morning's orange glow, is kissing the side wall of the building, highlighting the concrete blocks and making them stand out. The blocks emphasize the utilitarian aspect of the structure and suggest toughness. The wall is a great background for a portrait of the tough face of Knockemstiff. All we have to do is get that face into place before the light changes.

We quickly drive to the home of our contact, Bill Chaney, a World War II vet and lifelong resident of Knockemstiff. He has called on his cousin, Donald Pollack, for reinforcements. Noting Bill's unshaven face and somewhat menacing expression, I know we've found our man.

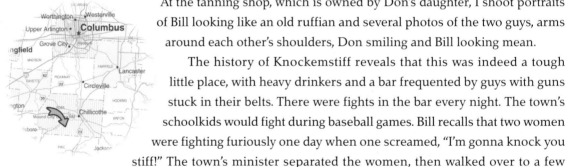

At the tanning shop, which is owned by Don's daughter, I shoot portraits of Bill looking like an old ruffian and several photos of the two guys, arms around each other's shoulders, Don smiling and Bill looking mean.

The history of Knockemstiff reveals that this was indeed a tough little place, with heavy drinkers and a bar frequented by guys with guns stuck in their belts. There were fights in the bar every night. The town's schoolkids would fight during baseball games. Bill recalls that two women were fighting furiously one day when one screamed, "I'm gonna knock you stiff!" The town's minister separated the women, then walked over to a few parishioners, rolled his eyes, and said, "Any more fighting in this town and we'll have to call it Knockemstiff, Ohio." The townspeople, who relished their community's outlaw reputation, thought that would be just fine.

KNOCKEMSTIFF

Ohio

Donald Pollack and Bill Chaney, cousins

On our way to Odd, West Virginia, we find ourselves in a cluster of strangely-named towns. According to the map we're within ten miles of Low Gap, Fancy Gap, Shoe, Hooker, Bottom, Max, The Lump, and Mayo Mountain, among others. It's so hot that I move the map off the hood of the Trooper and onto the grass at the side of the road because the heat coming off the car's hood is burning through the paper and scorching my elbows.

We cruise into Bottom and find an old general store that promises cold sodas. Inside we meet the owner, Tommy Bowman, an elderly gentleman with a severe stoop. Feeling around for the coldest can in the old-fashioned cooler case—the really frigid ones are always at the bottom where the coldest air collects—I ask him how Bottom got its name. He tells us it's so named because the town is at the bottom of a hollow, and surveyors used that description for the name when they made the area's map.

When we tell Tommy about our project and ask if he'll come outside and pose next to the store's stock of tomatoes and bananas, he's happy to oblige. While we're shooting a customer stops by, squeezes some fruit, eyes the camera and the reflector, and asks us what we're doing. I think, we're hitting bottom, but I don't say it.

BOTTOM
North Carolina
Tommy Bowman, general store proprietor

As we barrel across Washington, the snow-capped Cascades, bathed in bright sunlight, give way to rolling green high plains. Wind-driven tumbleweed darts across the interstate. We can understand why people who see this lovely country as first-time visitors often end up living here.

We follow our maps to where Dynamite should be. We find fields, a few scattered houses, and the freshly oiled dirt of Dynamite Road, but nothing else. No one is in sight, and we're cautious about knocking on someone's door. It's just too quiet, and two easterners with a yuppie sport utility vehicle might get run off with a shotgun. Then we see two people far away in a small corral. One is riding a horse, the other leaning on the fence.

The sun is getting low and the golden hour with the day's best light for photography is fast approaching. We locate a narrow dirt road that leads us near the corral. We drive slowly past the "No Trespassing" sign, ready to make quick apologies and a quicker slip into reverse gear. A barbed-wire fence brings us to a stop about fifty yards from the corral. The people stare. I wave. The rider, a young girl, waves back. I yell, "I'm looking for the town of Dynamite!" The other person, an older guy who looks like the Marlboro Man, walks over. He is Tony Byrne, the girl's father.

Two minutes into my story Tony agrees to take us to the ruins of the old stone building where the railroad stored dynamite in the early 1900s. The Chinese laborers who built the railroad were housed near that building, which was located in the wilderness in order to protect the local citizens in case of an explosion. Apparently the laborers were not considered important enough to be housed somewhere else. The shantytown that grew up around the stone storage shed was called Dynamite.

On horseback, Tony tells us to follow, and he rides off through the woods. I engage the Trooper's four-wheel drive and proceed with caution, bouncing over logs and stones and through pools of muddy water. After a quarter mile of driving along the old railroad tracks on the crushed stones, and praying that the twice-weekly train doesn't pick this moment to arrive, we get to the site of the storage building, which looks like half of it has been blown away. But the golden hour is here, and we're in the heart of Dynamite, so we fire off our film.

DYNAMITE

Washington

Tony Byrne, rancher

As the sun is diving for the hilltops of central Tennessee, we stop at a diner and country store in the town of Difficult. Inside, an entire family serves dinner to locals. We pay for our Cokes and are about to inquire about the town's name and ask the family to pose for us when they ask if we're from New York. Apparently they have spotted the license plate on the Trooper. I say yes and the questions started flying. Turns out they once lived way upstate, and even though true upstaters (known to city types as apple knockers) would never talk to Manhattanites, they treat us like ex-neighbors.

We go outside and photograph the whole family, but we feature the dad and his eleven-year-old daughter up front. He's got two tattoos and is wearing a bright-orange T-shirt. She's in a brand-new maroon cowboy hat and smiles from behind her dad's considerable girth as he's hugging her. The sun burns out as it sets behind the restaurant's roof.

We find out that the town's name stems from a Civil War battle. A Union brigade, camped in a wooded hollow, was desperately trying to find a rebel encampment they knew was nearby. Late at night they could hear the enemy troops, but navigating through the deep woods in darkness was almost impossible. In the daylight, unable to see campfires, they couldn't track the enemy. When a Union general asked about the progress of the unit's mission, he was told that the hilly and thickly wooded terrain was hard to scout in. "Where they're camped is difficult," he was told. The general said, "Well, you just get to Difficult and find them." Eventually they did find the rebel unit and defeated them in battle.

Today we've driven 350 miles and photographed in four towns. We take a grab shot of a beautiful sunset-streaked sky and then head for the next Best Western.

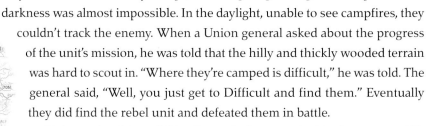

DIFFICULT

Tennessee

Leonard Levinsailor, market owner, and his daughter, Megan

On the narrow, straight road into Zap we pass a "drag line" pit, which is not a group of female impersonators waiting to dance, but rather a big open hole in the ground where miners take coal from the surface of the earth using huge buckets. The public-relations-minded coal company has set up a display of drag line buckets alongside the road for tourists to gape at and stand in. There's even a lonely sign on the road that proclaims the site a "point of interest." Of course we can't resist driving the Trooper into the mouth of the biggest bucket and taking pictures.

The mine truckers drive by in their mammoth ore-hauling trucks, which are as high as New York City brownstones. Each driver, a tiny speck in his cab, waves as he passes. We're in very friendly country here and, like little kids, we wave back.

It's very flat territory, but the tiny town of Zap is hidden from view behind a small hill. The town's major feature is a blue water tower that looks like a grain-storage silo because its walls enclose it from base to top. "ZAP" is painted in large letters on the side. A fence rolls slightly up and over the hill next to the tower. The scene looks high-plains lonely.

Zap is pretty much deserted. Not only are there many abandoned homes, but it's also the Saturday of a holiday weekend. We learn that the town is named after Zapp, a coal-mining village in Wales. And that's about all anyone seems to know about it.

We meet Jim Wills, a long-haul trucker, on the lawn of his modest house. He agrees to pose for us near the water tower. It's overcast and very windy when we set up and Jim's shirttails flap in the breeze. Twenty minutes and seven rolls later Jim signs a model release form and we start off on a long haul of our own to the next town.

ZAP

North Dakota

Jim Wills, long-haul trucker

Nobody knows for sure how the town got its name, but there is a story, made up by a local funeral director who got tired of the mayor asking him to answer letters from schoolchildren writing to ask about the name. The tale, which he printed up in a form letter to respond to inquiries, rambles on like the plot of a children's book. There was, he wrote, a circus monkey that escaped from a riverboat that caught fire. It took up residence in the trees of Paducah. Barely surviving the winters, the monkey lost all its hair. It was eventually adopted by a family who cared for it, and all its fur grew back except for one eyebrow.

There's another story about an organ grinder whose monkey had only one eye and an extra-bushy eyebrow over the empty socket.

But as we're driving to the shoot, I notice on the area map that a bend in the nearby Ohio River forms the exact shape of a monkey's head, with the town located on a tributary that's exactly where the eyebrow would be. It's so obvious we can't believe it. When we tell some of the locals they shrug and smile but seem to prefer their stories to our topographic discovery.

We photograph crane operator and part-time actor Bobby Hall in a tobacco field next to one of the town's signs. He tells us he's had walk-on parts on the *Walker, Texas Ranger* television series. He says they never cast good guys who were taller than Chuck Norris. He is filled with hope for a successful show business career. "I have a great agent in Chicago," he says, "but it's real hard getting parts while I'm still living out here in Monkey's Eyebrow."

Despite the heat and bugs, Bobby works at his posing like a pro as I shoot endless variations. I usually like to shoot until I get that "you done good, you got the shot" feeling, but it's 108 degrees out here so I just shoot until we're all worn out.

MONKEY'S EYEBROW

Kentucky

Bobby Hall, crane operator

t's a gray, rainy afternoon when we cross the one-lane bridge into the tiny hamlet of Lovely, where we're greeted by a big, white building with painted black letters that announce "Church of Lovely."

We had called the county offices and asked about the likelihood of finding a resident to pose for us. An elderly citizen, widowed last year, was suggested as someone who might have fun doing that.

We meet Mrs. Mary Martin at the neat little mobile home where she's been living since her house was destroyed in a fire earlier in the year. She is full of verve despite her recent misfortunes. In fact, she's anxious to show us how well she can navigate with her new hip joint, installed only a few months ago.

Mary remarks to me, "I would never do this except that Velma at the County says that you're OK." Then she pauses and asks, "You *are* OK, aren't you?" Yes, I am, I say, and, because Velma has vouched for me, I become extra protective of Mary.

She talks of her twenty grandchildren and great-grandchildren, showing us photo albums. She announces the names of each child pictured in the black-and-white snapshots, slowing occasionally to drift off in a memory. We ask her to bring one of her ten family photo albums as a prop for the shoot.

The next morning we arrive at the church an hour early to find the best position and take advantage of the great morning light. Mary arrives twenty minutes early, carrying her photo album. She is driven to the site by one of her grandsons, who tells us he learned photography in the Army.

I ask Mary if the white reflector we're using is too bright for her, and she says that she has already figured out that "if I keep my head down a little, it doesn't make me squint."

At the exact moment Mary looks absolutely great, a big dump truck streams blue smoke into the scene. All told, seven trucks interrupt seven wonderful moments. Fortunately, Mary is a woman of many wonderful moments.

LOVELY

Pennsylvania
Mary Martin, great-grandmother

Mars is a big enough town to have a historical society, but I begin to wonder about its reliability when I see the following inscription on the plaque outside the society's headquarters: "Mars was named after the star, Mars."

We find out from a resident that the town's main attraction is a ten-foot-in-diameter metal model of a flying saucer, placed by the historical society on a prime piece of downtown real estate. When we find the mini-craft parked where there might otherwise have been a statue of a founding father, we know we have our shooting location.

Next we find John Clutter, the man who painted the numbers on the spaceship. He agrees to pose. The evening light is nice and low, and the spaceship shines above the glowing backlit green grass.

As we are getting the model release form signed, John tells us that he's seen a real flying saucer in Mars. "It flew over town here one night," he says. "It had an orange glow and was very quiet. There seem to be a lot of sightings here." A friend of John's, standing nearby, nods his head. "I saw them, too," he says earnestly. "You know, they only let certain people see them."

I hasten the model release signing.

MARS

Pennsylvania
John Clutter, retired maintenance engineer

AT JOURNEYS' END

The totals:

- Over 38,000 miles covered in 9 trips in 5 years through 40 states.
- In 115 days on the road I burned 2,800 gallons of regular gas, shot 21,000 frames of film, stayed in 72 bad-smelling motels and 8 great ones, and ate 360 bad meals and 3 terrific ones.
- Number of times I took the Lord's name in vain in bad traffic situations: 271.
- Number of times He helped me out: 0.
- Number of times I impersonated a long-distance trucker on the CB radio to get police location reports: 15.
- Number of times I got caught doing this: 1.
- Number of car washes needed to de-bug the exterior of the Trooper: 18.
- Number of times I revised my assessment "This has got to be the world's worst cup of coffee ever!": 46.

Confessions due:

1. And this is it: When I set out I thought I'd be meeting a lot of cartoon characters in the strangely named towns I'd be visiting. But a funny thing happened: I found that real people live in those places, and they live in my photographs as well. They were people who greeted total strangers with kindness and even warmth. Yes, there were a few who were strange and one or two who were surly, but they were the rare exceptions. And even they weren't cartoon characters.

So sure was I that the people I'd meet would be guarded when they saw this city slicker that I armed myself with a mountain of credentials. I took letters of introduction from national magazines and noted publishers and household-name corporations. I took samples of the kinds of photos I was planning to shoot. I even printed up for my three-ring presentation notebook a fancy cover with the title *Unique America Project*—and wasn't that just warm and fuzzy enough to elicit the cooperation of strangers?

As it turned out, I didn't need any of it. Most of the people we approached smiled immediately with a knowing look to suggest that they agreed that their town's name rightfully deserved our attention.

One of the things I learned from the adventure was that I could become addicted to this kind of full-time wandering. Each trip was more fun than the last. Looking back at the faces and reading my notes makes me smile. It triggers the sound of voices, the smell of hot, oil-soaked dirt roads, the feel of cool raindrops. I remember the aromas of corn dirt and green leaves as a downpour freed the field's fragrances. I see again how smilingly radiant Mary Martin was despite her incredibly un-lovely year in Lovely. I realize that some older people are resilient in ways that are downright astounding. It's a good thing, because I'm planning on becoming one.

I learned too that New Yorkers are not universally considered barbarous. In a diner in a small town in Texas, the waitress, hearing our accents, asked where we were from. When I said New York, she whirled around to squeal to everybody else, "Oh, my God! I can't believe it! Why, I just served my very first New Yorkers!" She then sat down at our table to ask about life in the Big Apple, and we encouraged her to follow her dream and move to the city.

Once, getting directions driver-to-driver from a young man in a pickup truck on a dirt road in Odd, West Virginia, I was shocked when he lurched from his driver's seat toward my open window. I slapped down the door lock and hit the accelerator hard—a New Yorker's reaction. But he was reaching only to shake my hand in a boisterous gesture of friendship. Rattled and embarrassed, I navigated back to the highway.

Looking at the pictures after the trips, I saw warm, sweet, and earnest people. And funny and even zany ones. They seemed to like me. I know I liked them. I enjoyed their humor and sense of community. These folks were my partners in a struggle to make the most of what we'd been dealt.

What else I learned:

- People in Texas stop on the yellow light. To them it does not signify a grace period.
- Budget motels are barely in the service business. They make their profits from markups on phone calls.
- For those of you going there, Hell isn't so bad.
- Pedestrians in San Francisco scowl meaner than New Yorkers do when you invade their crosswalks with your bumper.
- Scenery in Oregon, Washington, and Idaho is as beautiful as advertised, and then some.
- Waitresses are sweet but never seem to marry the right guys.
- There isn't one good cup of strong coffee within ten miles of any interstate in America.
- In the Midwest the coffee looks good—just a little darker than tea, it photographs well—but it tastes like warm flood water.
- Every motel towel in rooms priced below $60 a night is rough enough to be used for stripping paint from furniture.
- For breakfast, Denny's rules.

- If you're lost in middle America, people will treat you like a neighbor. They will tell you things like, "Turn left up where the church used to be."
- When you stay in a different motel room every night for sixteen consecutive nights, always leave the bathroom light on when you go to sleep. Since every room has a different layout, this will save you a late-night visit to the closet.
- Truck drivers do not know where to eat.
- Cooking grease is a national condiment.
- It is required by most small-town governments that everything on the menu of the only restaurant open after 7:00 P.M. be fried food.
- Most Americans do not believe that anyone actually lives in Manhattan.
- Always place the motel's plastic drinking cup on the corner of the bathroom sink and weight it with the toothpaste tube and toothbrush. Otherwise it'll get knocked into the toilet many times.
- Hold the bottles that are inside the cooler firmly when tipping the cooler to empty melted ice onto the sidewalk. Otherwise, the bottles will fall out, break, and send grapefruit juice into your shoes.
- Finally, I learned that all those years ago, Walter wasn't talking crazy at all.